IMAGES OF

BATTLESHIPS WWII
EVOLUTION OF THE BIG GUNS

RARE PHOTOGRAPHS FROM WARTIME ARCHIVES

PHILIP KAPLAN

Pen & Sword
MARITIME

First printed in Great Britain in 2015 by
Pen & Sword Maritime
an imprint of
Pen & Sword Books Ltd.
47 Church Street
Barnsley,
South Yorkshire
S70 2AS

A CIP record for this book is available from the
British Library.

ISBN 978 1 78 346 3077

Printed and bound in Malta
By Gutenberg Press Ltd.

Pen & Sword Books Ltd incorporates the
Imprints of Pen & Sword Aviation, Pen & Sword
Family History, Pen & Sword Maritime, Pen &
Sword Military, Pen & Sword Discovery,
Wharncliffe Local History, Wharncliffe True
Crime, Wharncliffe Transport, Pen & Sword
Select, Pen & Sword Military Classics, Leo
Cooper, The Praetorian Press, Remember When,
Seaforth Publishing and Frontline Publishing.

For a complete list of Pen & Sword titles please
contact Pen & Sword Books Limited
47 Church Street, Barnsley, South Yorkshire, S70
2AS, England

E-mail: enquiries@pen-and-sword.co.uk
Website: www.pen-and-sword.co.uk

Contents

Reasonable efforts have been made to
trace the copyright holders of all material
used in this book. The author apologizes
for any omissions. All reasonable efforts
will be made in future editions to correct
any such omissions. The author is grateful
to the following people for the use of
their published and/or unpublished materi-
al, and for their kind assistance in the
preparation of this book: Charles Addis,
Tony Alessandro, Malcolm Bates,
Quentin Bland, Charles Brown, Shannon
Callahan, Phoebe Clapham, B.R. Coward,
Jack Delaney, Keith De Mello, Ernest
Ervin, Herb Fahr, Michael Fiske, James
Flecker, Joseph Gilby, Gregory Haines,
HMS Drake Photo Section, Earl
Haubrich, Mike Holloman, Eric Holloway,
Pamela Holmes, Tony Iacono, Jan Jacobs,
David Jones, Albert Lee Kaiss, Hargi
Kaplan, Margaret Kaplan, Neal Kaplan,
John Keegan, Richard Landgraff, Henry
Leach, Maynard Loy, Ted Mason, Richard
McCutcheon, Rita McCutcheon, F.W.
Meacham, David Mellor, Neil Mercer,
Richard Minear, Morris Montgomery,
Robert Oelrich, Ted Pederson, Bruce
Porter, Harold Porter, Ernie Pyle,
R.V. Racey, Henry Sakaida, Robert
Sambataro, John Shelton, Doug Siegfried,
Mike Sizeland, Robert Shultz, Ian Smith,
Mark Stanhope, Mark Thistlethwaite, John
Wellham, Stanley Vejtasa, Mitsuru Yoshida.

The launching of the USS *North Dakota*, BB29, at Quincy, Massachusetts in 1909. A dreadnought battleship of the *Delaware* class, she remained in the United States in a training capacity during the First World War, and took no part in actual combat in her career. She was decomommissioned in 1923 under the terms of the Washington Naval Treaty, was scrapped in 1931 and later dismantled. Armed with ten 12-inch main guns, she had a top speed of 21 knots.

AMERICAN PATROL

Words by EARL HAUBRICH
Music by F.W. MEACHAM

left: The USS *Missouri,* BB63, in the New York Navy Yard for a refit in July 1944. right: The USS *Alabama,* BB60, on the building ways at the Norfolk Navy Yard, Virginia. A *South Dakota* class vessel served in both the Atlantic and Pacific theaters of the Second World War. She was to become a museum ship at Mobile, Alabama in 1965.

The German battleship *Tirpitz*, sister ship of the *Bismarck*, was named after Grand Admiral Alfred von Tirpitz, who had planned the modern German Imperial Navy. She is shown in her fitting-out berth. She was commissioned in February 1941; below left: The launch of the German battleship *Bismarck* at Hamburg in February 1939; below right: The USS *New Jersey*, BB62, on Pacific duty in WW2.

The USS *Idaho*, BB24, fitting out in the William Cramp Yard at Philadelphia, Pennsylvania, in 1906. The second of the *Mississippi* class battleships, *Idaho* was sold to Greece and renamed *Lemnos* in 1914. She was sunk by German bombers in April 1941.

U.S.S. ALABAMA (BB60)
BOW VIEW AT FITTING OUT BERTH
NORFOLK NAVY YARD PORTSMOUTH VA
PHOTO SERIAL 10-174-50 JULY 3, 1942

The USS *Alabama* in her fitting out berth at Norfolk, Virginia, 1942

top: Lowering one of the great sixteen-inch main guns into a turret of the USS *North Carolina*, BB55, during her fitting out. Serving in every major naval action in the Pacific in WW2, she was the most highly-decorated U.S. battleship of the war; above: The main guns of the battleship USS *South Carolina*, BB26, in a scrapyard at Philadelphia, Pennsylvania, in 1923.

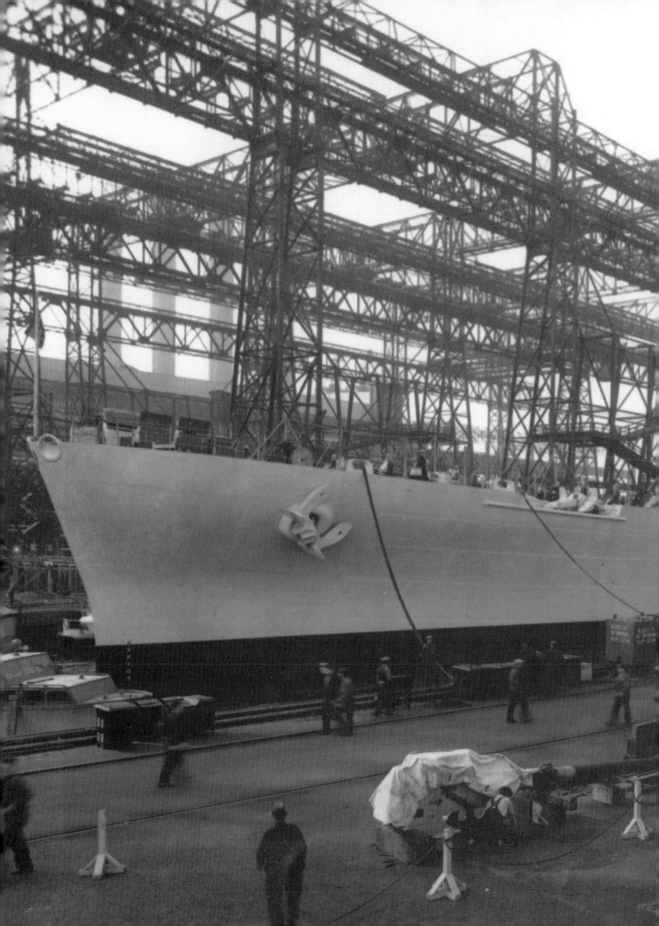

The newly-competed USS *North Carolina*, BB55, at the New York Navy Yard in 1941.

Battleship Sailors

Visitor's Day, 1918, at the Great Lakes Naval Training Station near Chicago, Illinois.

Battleship sailors, we get the big head. We're the best. In any competition with another ship, we come out on top. We work hard and the work is tedious. But when we pull into port, we look good. We know that.
—Ernest Ervin, Reidsville, North Carolina

I actually had some connection with all of the *King George V* battleships. When I first left Dartmouth [Britannia Royal Naval College] in January 1941, I was appointed to the *Prince of Wales*. In fact, I never joined her, because my father, who was then the Director of Naval Ordnance, came home at Christmas time for a short weekend and, although he wouldn't say where he was going, I had guessed correctly that he was going to become captain of the *Prince of Wales*, so I couldn't go there. I had a month in the *Rodney*, and I joined *Duke of York*, as a Sub-Lieutenant in the late summer of '42. I was president of the Gun Room Mess. My action station was in the fourteen-inch transmitting station (the computer room, as the

American navy called it), where I was on a thing called the spotting plot. The fall of shot was observed from the director control tower, right up aloft, passed by telephone to me on the spotting plot, and it fell to me to apply the necessary corrections to either continue to straddle the target, or to move so that you did straddle the target.
—Admiral of the Fleet Sir Henry Leach, HMS *Duke of York*

Ted Pederson served aboard the 'Big Mo' (USS *Missouri*) from October 1948 to August 1950, in the Deck Division as a hot-shellman on the left gun of five-inch mount Number Ten. "Early in 1949 I transferred to the Radar Division where I stood watches in radar, learning the job, operating different radars, radar navigation and plotting. After going to radar school, I returned to the 'Mo' and was ordered to stand my first watch on the conn, or bridge.

"The radar watch on the bridge stood right next to the captain's chair on the starboard side and operated a radar repeater. This watch functioned as the captain's "eyes", ready to answer questions from the captain or the Officer of the Deck, about other vessels, navigation points, range and bearings, and questions to and from Radar or the Combat Information Center. The uniform of the day was whites and I had made sure that I looked sharp in my starched whites and nicely shined shoes. It being my first watch, I was nervous.

"On the bridge, it was all business. Nobody talked unless it was necessary. Nobody smoked or drank coffee except the captain or the Officer of the Deck. Our skipper at the time was Captain Harold Page Smith Jr., a really good man, the type of man most sailors wanted for a skipper. One of his mottos was 'A clean ship is a happy ship.' We were the happiest ship in the fleet. When I assumed my watch on the bridge, the skipper was not yet there, but early into my watch he came and sat in his chair.

"Captain Smith was a smoker. So was I. He lighted a cigarette and when he exhaled, I inhaled. It did not take long for him to notice this action on my part. The skipper asked me if I smoked and I replied, 'Yes, sir.' He then reached into his shirt pocket, withdrew a pack of Camels, shook a cigarette out and asked me if I wanted one. Dying for a smoke, of course I wanted one and I took it. The captain was even kind enough to give me a light. Moments later he left his chair. I thought we really had a good skipper who looked out for his men. Crewmen were not supposed to smoke on the bridge and here was the captain giving me a cigarette. Moments after the skipper left his chair, while I was enjoying my cigarette, the Officer of the Deck spotted me smoking. He screamed my name and asked me 'What the hell do you think you're doing smoking on the bridge?' All I could say was 'But, but, but . . .' After a few minutes of real good ass-chewing, the skipper came back to his chair, laughing. He told the OD that he gave me the cigarette. Of course, by that time I had stomped on the cigarette. Captain Smith asked me if I had learned anything. I think I was too dumbstruck to reply, but after the watch I made up my mind to never accept a smoke on the bridge, not even from an admiral. There were no hard feelings from the captain. He had just played a joke and had a little fun with a member of his crew.
—Ted Pederson, USS *Missouri*

Nineteen-year-old Seaman First Class Tony Iacono was a gun-pointer in mount four, a five-inch gun mount on the battleship USS *New Jersey* in 1944. "We used to have a gunshack on the port superstructure, for the gunner's mates on the port side. It was right next to a vent

left: The battleships USS *Colorado*, BB45, and *West Virginia*, BB48, seen from the USS *Iowa* in Japan, October 1945; at bottom: Seaman First Class Tony Iacono was a gun-pointer in Mount Four, a five-inch gun on the USS *New Jersey*, BB62, in 1944.

that sucked hot air out of the bowels of the ship. We used to plug that up with blankets so that the chefs would sweat. Then they would come up and say 'Hey, what's happening?' And then we would trade with them. We would take the blankets out of the vent in exchange for their bringing us a tray of cake.

"When we came into port, either at Ulithi or Mog Mog, we would get a ration of 3.2 beer. We would go ashore and play baseball. The winning side would drink all the beer, which was warm."

"It was January 1991. We had been in the Persian Gulf for a few weeks and the war between the U.S. and Iraq had just started. I was Boatswain's Mate of the watch, midnight to four a.m. I had all of my men placed on the other watches and had made sure they were there on time to relieve the off-going watches.

"I was standing at my station on the port side of the bridge and was recording an entry into the Boatswain's Mate book. I had sent my runner below decks for something. I noticed that there was someone wearing a black peacoat standing beside me. It was a cold night and we were all wrapped up good and warm. I saw this person from the corner of my eye as I wrote in the book. I figured he was one of the quartermasters just hanging out, wanting to strike up a conversation. I had a feeling of 'comfort' the whole time he was there. It was a feeling like you had when you were a kid and your dad was really proud of you for something.

"I turned towards the figure standing beside me . . . and he wasn't there. I wasn't frightened at all. It was eerie in a way though, but in a good way.

"After the watch that night, at about four in the morning, I was going below decks from the bridge, behind the quartermaster's area. I was about to open a hatch to pass through, when the hatch door opened by itself. I thought that someone was on the other side and coming my way. I stepped through the hatch and there was no one there. Then the door shut behind me and dogged itself."
—John E. Shelton, USS *Missouri*

'My GQ station turned out to be in the first compartment forward on 'Broadway' which is a long corridor down the middle of the ship right above the main engine and fire rooms. The 'Mo' had four fire rooms to make steam for the four engine rooms. So there were eight compartments along Broadway and mine was the first forward over the number one fire room. Entry to 'After Diesel' was just aft of the number four engine room, so, when GQ sounded, I had all eight compartments to run through to get to my battle station. Aboard ship, compartments are separated by watertight doors, which are kind of oval-shaped. The doors have a rubber strip around them and, when closed, match up with a 'knife-edge' going around the doorway. Along Broadway, the bottom of the doors was about eighteen inches above the deck, and when you were moving to your GQ station, you were moving fast and sometimes your shin would not quite make it over the bottom of the door, and, bam-scrape, another hatch scar. I still have those scars today."
—Herb Fahr, USS *Missouri*

Few officers on assuming command realise to what extent their personality is mirrored in the ship. Every word which you say on the bridge is noted by the ship's company. Every word which you say in the wardroom is marked by the officers. A display of unwarranted temper on the bridge, an unjust or over-hasty reprimand, a careless piece of shiphandling, an uncloaked show of anxiety, all these incidents will be reflected by your officers and men just as the planets reflect the light of the sun. Similarly, a disregard of danger on the bridge carries courage to every corner of the ship.

Experience in the fleet has shown that a large number of serious offences could have been avoided if the Captain's Standing Orders, particularly those concerning rum, and the inspection of libertymen returning from leave, had been more concisely written, and more rigidly applied.

The supply and issue of rum needs a Commanding Officer's keenest supervision. It is essential that an officer attends daily issue, and checks most carefully the supply and opening of new casks. Supply Ratings will only fall to the temptation of misappropriation of the falsifying of accounts if they know that the officers are out of touch with the situation.
—from *Your Ship: Notes and Advice to an Officer on Assuming His First Command*, 1944 [Royal Navy]

In the mid-1930s, a little fox terrier named *At'Em* was made a member of the crew of the USS *Arizona*. He was issued his own Navy serial number and liberty card.

"We had been in and out of Guantanamo Bay, Cuba, during the stormy season and were on our way back to Guantanamo. I was on watch on the bridge and overheard this exchange. We were on a direct heading for the bay entrance and going at a pretty good clip of around twenty-five to thirty knots. The wind had increased to a high velocity. We had picked up a line of U.S. Navy destroyers off our starboard side at about 10,000 yards or five miles. They were on a collision course with us, which is where the bearing remains constant and the range continues to decrease. I informed the skipper, Captain H.P. Smith. When the range between us and the lead tin can had reached about three and a half miles, Commander George Peckham, the Executive Officer, came on the bridge and stated rather loudly, 'Captain, there's a fleet of tin cans off our starboard bow on a collision course.' The skipper replied, 'I see them, George.' A few minutes later, the Exec returned to the bridge and announced, 'Captain, the fleet of tin cans on our starboard bow is still on a collision course.' The skipper replied, 'I see them, George.' The Exec then left the bridge.

"Moments later, the lead destroyer was about 2,500 yards away and the Exec returned to the bridge to announce quite loudly, 'Captain, we are on a collision course with that lead tin can. The Executive Officer recommends we reduce speed and change course to avoid!' The skipper looked at the Exec and replied, 'George, you tell the Executive Officer that I am the skipper of this ship and I outrank every skipper on those tin cans, and besides that, I'm bigger!' We did not change course or speed. The tin cans backed down, not us. Word got around the ship about this exchange. The crew liked our skipper a lot more."
—Ted Pederson, USS *Missouri*

"Life in the old Navy was no picnic. Below decks, the short battleship USS *Maryland* looked like a beehive, with over 2,000 men in the ship's company. Crewmen could not have cameras and they could not go topside. For most of the four years that I was on board the

Maryland, crew members could only be at their living quarters, their General (combat) Quarters, or perhaps have the luxury of a pass to visit the ship's barber. On the *Maryland*, the crew slept in hammocks. They had bins for mess tables and they ate in the same compartment where they slept."
—Harold Porter, USS *Maryland*

"We never took our clothes off at sea, except odd times when we would sneak a quick wash

left: A much-tattooed sailor in the USS *New Jersey* in 1944; below: A *New Jersey* gunner loading powder bags.

all over. For sleep, any locker, table top or mess stool—one could sleep on anything, even if only about four inches wide."
—R.V. Racey, RN, from *Battleship, Cruiser, Destroyer* by Gregory Haines and Commander B.R. Coward, RN

"We knew about the war coming and we painted the ship a dull black, instead of the gray. They tried that out. The plan of the day would come out and it would say ALL HANDS

REPORT FOR PHYSICAL DRILL FOLLOWED BY GUNNERY DRILL. We had that every day except Saturday and Sunday."
—Richard McCutcheon, USS *West Virginia*

The final and most important temptation which confronts every Commanding Officer is the same as that which has brought so many dictators to the ground. 'Power corrupts' is a dictum which does not only apply to politics. Bernard Shaw has recently enlarged on this by stating 'Power corrupts the weak and dements the strong.' As a Commanding Officer you are an autocrat pure and simple, and you are subject to the same temptations as an autocrat. No one in your ship can check your excesses, or point out your eccentricities; no one can question your downright assertions; everyone must endure your temper or any other foible you may develop. You are treated with the deference and ceremony not always granted to a cabinet minister.

All this has the effect of accentuating your weaknesses, unless you watch yourself most carefully. Only some candid and regular introspection will keep you in command of yourself. The forces which turned Captain Bligh into a tyrant, though perhaps weaker, are still extant. Bligh was in many ways a good character; he was an efficient officer and a competent seaman; he possessed great courage and powers of endurance; but he had insufficient strength of will to repress two instincts, which are normally repressed in youth. He submitted himself to unbridled temper, and to sadism. The modern laws of the Navy rightly do not tolerate a practical application of the latter, but do not forget that it is within your power to cause considerable mental anguish to your younger officers by a consistent tone of sarcasm and contempt, and that, after the undue strain and fatigue of command in warfare, it is quite simple to submit to such childish intolerance over small and petty irritations. And what is worse, nobody is going to tell you about them. In all officers, but above all in Commanding Officers, the words Officer and Gentleman should be entirely synonymous.
—from *Your Ship, Notes and Advice to an Officer on Assuming His First Command*, 1944 (Royal Navy)

"I ate that chow for three years. We had beans Monday, Wednesday and Saturday, three times a day. We had a lot of Spam, a LOT of Spam. We had all the coffee we wanted, made in big urns. During General Quarters there was no chow. When we were under attack, we didn't eat. When the attack was over, the first thing we had to do was clean up the guns, get rid of the hot cases and get ready for the next battle. After that, you ate when it was time for your side to eat.

"Some of that food, for a guy who came from a small town in the middle west, I couldn't eat it. It didn't even look good. But some of those guys just sloshed it down like it was good. Some of that stuff they used to make for us was streaky, watery, gooey stuff we used to call Slumgullion. It didn't even look fit to eat. There was no ketchup, no butter, and no ice on the table. They made their own bread, with a lot of weevils in it. We used to hold the bread up to the light and count the bogies in it. Sometimes there would be ten or twelve dead weevils in it. And then, when there was foul weather, and the cooks couldn't cook because the sea was too rough, we used to get bologna sandwiches. I used to fill my locker up with sandwiches because I never got seasick. The chow on the ship was good when you were in port,

overleaf: Survivors of the sunken battleship *Bismarck* struggle in the sea awaiting rescue; below: The first iron-clad warship of the United States Navy, *Monitor*, commissioned during the American Civil War; bottom: On board the Royal Navy's HMS *Britannia* in 1904.

but when you were at sea, it was . . . whatever you could get. There was one time when we were at sea for sixty days and we got beans all the time because they ran out of everything.

"We used to pick up Tokyo Rose when we were standing watch at night. She played all the nice music: Glenn Miller, Benny Goodman, Tommy Dorsey, all the good songs. You're on watch at four in the morning, you can't go to sleep, you can't even sit down. You've got to stand up. One night she said, 'Today we sank the Blue Dragon (the Japanese used to call our ship the Blue Dragon), and we'd laugh like hell. She was always saying things like, 'You know, your wife or girlfriend is out with your neighbour. She's cheating on you.' Always planting bad thoughts in your mind.

"I used to gamble and sometimes I'd win. Craps or cards. And I'd send money home to my father because I knew that the house wasn't paid for. I said, 'Pay for the house.' I didn't know how much I sent. So, when I came back from the service, he handed me a checkbook with over $3,000 in it. I said, 'What's this?' He said, 'That's your money. That's the money you sent your mother to pay for the house. Now this is your money, if you want to use it to get married, go to school or buy a car . . . nothing else. You can't waste it.' So, I wound up buying a car".
—Tony Iacono, USS *New Jersey*

General messing—all catering done by the Paymaster and his staff. The food in general was very good, the only dish which few would eat was tripe and onions. It usually went straight from the galley to the gash.
—A.W.R. Brown, RN, from *Battleship, Cruiser, Destroyer* by Gregory Haines and Commander B.R. Coward, RN

"We left Cuba and the order came down to put on flank speed, which was about thirty-three knots or thirty-eight land miles per hour, the highest speed that the ship could steam. The fantail was awash with the four screws digging into the water with 180,000 horsepower on her shafts. Down in the after diesel, the four shafts passed through that space and were turning at a furious rate. We made Norfolk in about eight hours and got to our regular berthing space at pier seven in time for liberty call. We were home again."
—Herb Fahr, USS *Missouri*

The Navy had installed a square white porcelain bathtub in the captain's in-port cabin of the USS *Iowa* for President Franklin D. Roosevelt's trip to Casablanca in November 1943. Roosevelt, crippled by polio, was unable to use standard shipboard showers. Seaman First Class Leo Sicard was assigned to push Roosevelt around and help the president. Sicard recalled: 'He was a real sailor, and knew his way around. I was frightened by my responsibility, but was comforted when Mr Roosevelt said, 'I'm a human being, just the same as you.'

As well as the individual acquaintance of your men, you must know the 'atmosphere' of the ship. You must be close enough in touch with your ship's company to know of any feeling or rumour in the ship which may be a bad influence; for it is your job to dispel such impressions.

That your men should know you is equally important. They must know you well enough

American battleship sailors of the Second World War; bottom right: A massive bow wave created by the USS Iowa, BB61.

to look upon you as the trustee of their welfare on board and in their homes. Men are proverbially shy about putting in requests to see officers, and particularly the captain. You must make it clear to the men that not only their Divisional Officers, but you yourself will do all you can for their welfare. One of the instinctive desires in every man's mind is for security. If the sailors know that you are watching over their home security you will have gone a long way towards getting a happy ship.

The men will also know you indirectly in the way you handle the ship and exert your

influence to bring the ship to a high standard, but it is during your ship's company talks that each and every man will get to know you best. For that reason you must look upon your talks to the crew as one of the most important things you do. The first point to realise on these occasions is that you are talking to a body of men, a number of whom are quite intelligent, and that it is the intelligent ones, and not the dull ones, who are going to criticise your speech afterwards. Therefore, while talking in simple language, you must never talk down to the men. Neither imagine that you will get the best out of a crew which you never address.

An intelligent man wants both information and inspiration. For this reason the Silent Skipper of last-century fiction, who in some way gained the devotion of his men by never uttering a word, will not be a success today. At the same time, a sailor does not want to be mustered on someone else's mess deck to hear a succession of vague and long-winded discourses on nothing in particular. Neither does he enjoy false heroics or "flannel." Like his tot, the sailor prefers his talks neat. For this reason, when you talk, do it at a convenient time when everybody will hear. Make certain, also, that you have something quite definite to say, and work out exactly how to say it beforehand. If Winston Churchill has to rehearse all his speeches, there is no reason why you should not.

Bring in all you can about ships' movements without compromising security. If you have been in action, explain all you can, giving praise where due. If you have been in any large operation, use it to give the men a wider outlook, and foster a feeling of trust and admiration in the Commander-in-Chief and other senior officers.

Finally, when addressing a ship's company, be yourself. You cannot consistently go on being someone else for the whole commission. The sailors want to be commanded by a character, not a character sketch.
—from *Your Ship, Notes and Advice to an Officer on Assuming His First Command*, 1944 (Royal Navy)

The two officers scrambled out on the gunwale. The vast flat steel wall of the battleship's side confronted them. It towered like a skyscraper and stretched away, seemingly for blocks, on either side, hiding the atoll. Maryk leaped to the landing platform, a small square wooden grill bleached by salt water at the bottom of the steep gangway ladder. Keefer followed. 'Lie off and wait for us,' the exec shouted to Meatball. They mounted the ladder, jingling the guy chains. The OOD was a short, round-faced lieutenant-commander, grey at the temples, wearing very clean, very starched khakis. Maryk asked for the location of the flag officer. The OOD briskly gave him directions. The Caine officers left the quarterdeck and walked slowly aft, looking around at the majestic main deck of the New Jersey.

It was another world; and yet, somehow, the same world as the Caine, transfigured. They were on a forecastle, with anchor chains, wildcat, pelican hooks and bits, with ventilators and life lines. But the New Jersey's pelican hook was as big as the Caine's main guns; one link of the battleship's anchor chain would have stretched across the minesweeper's entire bow; and the main battery, the long, long cannons with their turrets, seemed bigger than the whole Caine. There were sailors and officers everywhere, the same crowd of blue and sprinkling of khaki, but the sailors were clean as Sunday-school boys, and the officers looked like their teachers, grown up and fussily neat. The great central cathedral of bridge and stacks jutted out of the deck skyward, a pyramid of metal, nervous with anti-aircraft batteries and radars; the deck dwindled aft beyond it for hundreds of feet. The New Jersey was awesome.
—from *The Caine Mutiny* by Herman Wouk

Armoured hatches were a hazard in harbour, but could be even worse at sea when one waited for the roll of the ship to help bias the weight in favour of either closing or opening the hatches, which were actuated by massive springs. There were several nasty accidents to

feet and hands.
—W. Burley, RN, from *Battleships, Cruisers, Destroyers* by Gregory Haines and Commander B.R. Coward, RN

"We stopped off at the Hollywood USO for some coffee and doughnuts, and chatted with some of the hostesses. One of them came up with some tickets for a TV show and we decided to go. It was the popular 'Truth or Consequences' show with Jack Bailey as MC. We got there early and got seats in the front row. As they do in these shows, they always have a sub-host come out and 'warm-up' the audience. The show was to be taped for showing an hour later. It always opened with the audience laughing it up a lot. What were they laughing at? On this particular show, it was me. In order to get the audience to laugh, the sub-host picked out a soldier and a sailor from the audience to come down to the stage. We were asked our names and where we were from, and I got a word in about being stationed on the 'Mo' and that got a round of applause. We were then asked who we thought could get dressed faster, men or women. Of course, the GI and I both said men. So, to prove it, the sub-host brought out two suitcases. One held women's clothes, the other one, men's. We were to see how fast we could get dressed. We each chose a suitcase. I got the women's clothes.

"Now it was a matter of timing. The show was about to begin. The announcer was getting ready when the GI and I got the signal to start dressing, and that was all that was needed. I attacked the suitcase and threw on some panties about six sizes too large and, with a prompt

Writing a letter home on the USS *Pennsylvania*, BB38, in 1941.

above: A World War One American recruiting effort; right: A post-WWI image of sailors from USS *Texas*, BB35.

A U.S. Navy rescue launch in Pearl Harbor after the Japanese surprise attack, 7 December 1941.

from the sub-host, I started pulling a girdle over my head. This brought howls from the audience, and that was what was being taped when the show was being introduced. The GI and I were shuffled under the seating area, took off the clothes we had put on and, with a well-done from the sub-host, we were both handed an envelope and escorted back to our seats. When the show was over my buddies gathered around me to find out what was in the envelope. I opened it and there were four one-dollar bills, a note and a gift certificate. The note said the four dollars was to pay the taxes for the prize on the gift certificate which was for a Zenith Transoceanic Portable radio, the envy of everyone during the 1950s. The radio could be picked up at the studio tours gift shop, which at that time was closed.

"So, we left the studio and went across the street to a bar where we asked the bartender to put the TV on for us so we could watch the show we had attended, and I bought the beer with the four dollars. When the show came on, I saw the audience laughing at the GI and myself, and as the camera panned around, my buddies showed up, laughing with the rest of them.

"The next day we toured the beaches in the hope of seeing some stars. We enjoyed the sight of thousands of bodies in skimpy bikinis. We hit all the famous beaches and the municipal pier at Santa Monica. I also ran up to the TV studio and picked up my prize radio. I was to enjoy it but a short time as it was stolen soon after. Anyway, it was a fun and relaxing liberty."
—Herb Fahr, USS *Missouri*

In April 1924, a woman named Madeline Blair managed to stow away aboard the USS *Arizona*, when the battleship was berthed in New York City. While the ship was under way to her next port of call, San Pedro, California, a scandal erupted when the stowaway was discovered. It transpired that the lady had been providing favours to the sailors who helped conceal her presence for nearly a month. Twenty-three sailors were tried and sentenced to naval prison terms of up to ten years. Miss Blair was transferred to a commercial vessel which returned her to New York.

But the standing toast that pleased the most / Was: The wind that blows, the ship that goes, And the lass that loves a sailor!
—*The Round Robin*

Each ship has its own baseball cap. It is a working cap, but has transcended its origin to become a non-official part of the uniform.

The dragon-green, the luminous, the dark, the serpent-haunted sea.
—from *The Gates of Damascus, West Gate*, by James Elroy Flecker

Shh! Don't talk too much. Shh! Don't know too much. Jack, don't be too hip, 'Cause a slip of the lip might sink a ship.
—unattributed

He has not even seen you, he / Who gave you your mortality; And you, so small, how can you guess / His courage or his lovliness. Yet in my quiet mind I pray / He passed you on the darkling way—/ His death, your birth, so much the same—/ And holding you, breathed once your name.
—*War Baby* by Pamela Holmes

Chief Petty Officer Robert Sambataro served aboard the USS *Missouri* as a medical corpsman during the Korean War: "Among the ships under United Nations command was HMCS *Cayuga*. I recall that they asked for medical supplies. What I didn't know then was that the medical officer was the famous imposter Ferdinand 'Fred' Demera. We both came from Lawrence, Massachusetts.

"There have been several accounts about the various careers of Demera. He took on several guises, among them zoologist, law student, teacher, and assistant prison warden. But surely his crowning achievement was that of surgeon-lieutenant aboard the *Cayuga*.

"Demera studied all of the medical books on board and performed dental surgery on the captain. He also looked after the wounded that were brought aboard. How did this come about? He became a friend of a New Brunswick doctor, J.C. Cyr. He stole Cyr's medical certificates and used Cyr's name when applying to join the navy. The navy was eager to have him, and since there was no medical examination and no fingerprinting, he was accepted in no time flat.

"His exploits aboard the ship made great press, but the end came for Demera when Dr Cyr in New Brunswick said that he was the real Dr Cyr. Demera was given $1,000. in back pay and deported to the U.S. No charges were filed. He died in 1982 after having been ordained a Baptist minister."

The USS *Missouri* is the last of a line of warships called Missouri. The first of these was a steam-powered and wooden side-wheeled frigate completed in 1942. She had two paddle wheels and was armed with two ten-inch guns and eight eight-inch guns. On 26 August 1943, a crewman dropped a demijohn of spirits of turpentine in a store room. A fire ignited and spread so rapidly that containment was not possible. In a few hours, the burnt-out hulk sank. More than 200 of her crew were rescued by the British ship-of-the-line *Malabar*.

The second *Missouri* was an iron-clad center-wheel steam sloop of the Confederate States of America. She was launched in April 1963 and was used mainly to transport workers around the coast of Louisiana. At the end of the Civil War, she was surrendered to the U.S. Navy.

The first warship to bear the name Missouri was launched 28 December 1901 and was a 12,362-ton battleship with a complement of forty officers and 521 men. She was armed with four twelve-inch guns, sixteen six-inch guns and a variety of smaller weapons. While engaged in target practice on 13 April 1904, a flare-back from one of her guns ignited a fire causing more than a thousand pounds of gunpowder to burn. Many of the ship's spaces quickly filled with deadly gas which suffocated five officers and twenty-nine men.

In December 1907, this *Missouri* was among sixteen white-painted battleships to pass in review before President Theodore Roosevelt at Hampton Roads, Chesapeake Bay. The Great White Fleet then departed on a celebrted fourteen-month world cruise. She later served as a training ship and, in June and July 1912, helped protect American lives at Guantanamo Bay during the Cuban Revolution. She served as a training vessel with the Atlantic Fleet during World War One, as well as transporting troops to and from France. She was scrapped in January 1922, under the terms of the Washington Naval Arms Limitation Treaty.

The final battleship *Missouri*, BB63, was commissioned on 11 June 1944. Speaking at her launch ceremonies, Senator Harry S. Truman said: "The time is surely coming when the people of Missouri can thrill with pride as the *Missouri* and her sister ships, with batteries blazing, sail into Tokyo Bay."

The USS *Arizona* memorial in Pearl Harbor, from the USS *Missouri*.

The New Capital Ship

left: The British aircraft HMS *Illustrious* dwarfed byt the supercarrier USS *John C. Stennis*, in the Persian Gulf.

"If we rebuild the battle fleet and spend many millions on doing so, and then war comes and the airmen are right, and all our battleships are rapidly destroyed by air attack, our money will have been largely thrown away. But if we do not rebuild it and war comes, and the airmen are wrong and our airmen cannot destroy the enemy's capital ships, and they are left to range with impunity on the world's oceans and destroy our convoys, then we shall lose the British Empire."
—Royal Navy Admiral of the Fleet Sir Ernie Chatfield to Lord Halifax

The Commander-in-Chief of the Combined Japanese Fleet, Admiral Isoroku Yamamoto, had been educated at Harvard University in Boston, Massachusetts. He had served Japan as its Naval Attaché in Washington and was well informed about the military strengths and capabilities of the United States.

As the beginning of World War Two in the Pacific loomed, Yamamoto had no illusions about America as an adversary and did not favour such a war, but he accepted its inevitability. He also believed that Japan could not win a long, drawn-out war with the United States. Yamamoto was convinced that Japan must "give a fatal blow to the enemy at the outset, when it was least expected." He was certain that anything less than the total destruction of the U.S. fleet "would awaken a sleeping giant."

Hector Bywater, a British naval authority had published a book in 1921, *Sea Power in the Pacific*, and by the following year it had become required reading at Japan's Naval War College and her Imperial Naval Academy. Bywater believed that distance, and the effort connected with secondary fuel and supply consumption, meant that the Japanese home islands were essentially protected from direct assault by American forces. With impressive foresight, he predicted that the only workable strategy for an American assault on Japan would require a massive island-hopping campaign, through the Marianas and then on to Guam and the Philippines. Following the success of *Sea Power in the Pacific*, Bywater published a second book, *The Great Pacific War*, in which he argued that Japan could achieve the goal of making her empire invulnerable by mounting a successful surprise attack on the U.S. fleet, followed by an invasion of Guam and the Philippines and by the fortification of her mandate islands. Bywater and Yamamoto met for an evening at London's Grosvenor House during the admiral's 1934 trip to Europe. In the meeting, Yamamoto expressed his profound interest in Bywater's theories and their possible implications for Japan.

The creation of the Greater East Asia Co-Prosperity Sphere—that was how the Japanese referred to their intended conquest of Southeast Asia in the late 1930s. They had already conquered Manchuria and then invaded mainland China. These adventures caused the United States to impose an embargo on Japan which covered war materials, scrap iron, steel, and aviation fuel. All Japanese assets in the U.S. were frozen as well. Japan had few natural resources and now her sources for strategic commodities were drying up. Her militarist rulers knew that, to survive and to win in China, they had to have the tin, bauxite, rubber and oil of Malaya and the Dutch East Indies. They saw war with the British Empire, the Dutch government in exile, and the United States as inevitable, and began planning attacks on American air bases in the Philippines and the U.S. Pacific Fleet at Pearl Harbor, Hawaii. The complete destruction of these targets would be necessary to clear the way for Japanese forces to conquer Malaya, the East Indies and China. They called upon Admiral Yamamoto to

HMS *Illustrious* is one of three *Invincible* class light aircraft carriers built for the Royal Navy in the late 1970s. After participating in the Falklands conflict, *Illustrious* served in operations in Iraq, Bosnia and Sierra Leone. In 2010, her Sea Harrier II aircraft were retired from service and she has since operated as a helicopter carrier.

far left: Admiral Isoroku Yamamoto; left: Japanese torpedo carrier-based torpedo bombers; below: U.S. Navy's Pensacola, Florida base in the 1930s.

right: U.S. Navy Fleet Admiral Chester Nimitz; centre far left: Taranto pilot John Wellham; far left bottom: U.S. Navy fighter ace Stanley Vejtasa; bottom centre: Douglas Aircraft assembly line for SBD dive-bombers in World War Two; below: Women war workers in an aircraft plant during the WW2.

devise, plan and implement the spectacular early Sunday morning surprise attack on the American battleships and facilities in Pearl Harbor on 7 December 1941. The admiral was known as "the father of Japanese naval aviation", and had led the campaign to develop his nation's aircraft carrier fleet. In January 1941 he began planning the Pearl Harbor raid.

Yamamoto's lingering misgivings about attacking the United States resurfaced as the date of the raid approached. He realized that a number of the U.S. Navy's key warships would not be in port at Pearl, as they were either in transit between the U.S. west coast and Hawaii, or re-fitting on the west coast. Additionally, the American aircraft carriers in the Pacific, *Lexington* and *Enterprise*, were operating at sea, and *Saratoga* was in port on the west coast. Yamamoto now knew it would not be possible to wipe out the U.S. Pacific Fleet in a single blow and that an essential second strike on the remains of the enemy fleet would have to be mounted within six months of the Pearl attack.

Admiral Yamamoto was inspired by the successful Royal Navy air attack on battleships and other warships of the Italian Navy at Taranto in November 1940. Bomb and torpedo-bearing Swordfish biplanes had crippled much of their enemy's fleet with one strike in the shallow waters of that port facility. The admiral noted similarities between the facilities of Pearl and Taranto and considered them in his initial planning of the raid. He determined that, for such an attack to succeed, he would require a thirty-one-ship task force including six aircraft carriers, *Akagi, Hiryu, Kaga, Shokaku, Soryu,* and *Zuikaku*, to approach within 200 miles of the Hawaiian Islands where they would likely encounter heavy enemy defences in the form of at least 100 fighter aircraft and the anti-aircraft guns of up to sixty-eight warships.

Pearl Harbor lies adjacent to the large airfield complex of Hickam Field and the Honolulu Airport. The harbour itself is a relatively shallow basin surrounding a small airfield known as Ford Island, and there is only one narrow channel leading from the harbour to the Pacific Ocean. On the eastern shore lay a submarine base, oil storage tanks and drydocks. At anchor on the southeast side of the harbour on the day of the attack were eight battleships of the American fleet, *Arizona, California, Maryland, Nevada, Oklahoma, Tennessee, Utah* and *West Virginia.* Another battleship, *Pennsylvania*, lay in a nearby drydock where she was being repaired. These warships would become the principal targets of the Japanese air strike.

Yamamoto's plan called for the Imperial Japanese Fleet to be assembling near the Kurile Islands, north of Japan on 22 November. On that day Japan's pair of special envoys in Washington, Admiral Kichisaburo Nomura and Saburo Kurusu, reported that they had made no progress in their attempts to resolve the differences between the two nations. Japan's militarists decided, therefore, that diplomacy had failed and directed their task force to head east from the Kuriles on 25 November. Escorted by battleships, cruisers, destroyers and submarines, the six Japanese carriers crossed much of the western Pacific, observing strict radio silence in an effort to reach the area north of the Hawaiian Islands without being detected by the enemy.

On 7 December 1941, the Japanese ambassador to Washington asked for an appointment to see the American Secretary of State, Cordell Hull, at 1 p.m. The Ambassador later telephoned and asked that the appointment be postponed to 1:45 as he was not quite ready for the meeting. He arrived at 2:05 and was received by Hull at 2:20 p.m.

The Japanese Ambassador stated that he had been instructed to deliver at 1 p.m. the doc-

below: A Grumman Avenger torpedo bomber crash-lands on the USS *Philippine Sea;* bottom left: U.S. Navy carrier pilots in their ready room during WW2; bottom right: U.S. Marine Corps night-fighter ace Colonel R. Bruce Porter.

ument which he then handed to the Secretary, and said that he was sorry that he had been delayed owing for the need for more time to decode the message. The Secretary asked why the Ambassador had specified one o'clock. The Ambassador replied that he did not know, but that that was his instruction. The Secretary noted that he was receiving the message after two o'clock.

After reading the first few pages, the Secretary asked the Ambassador whether the document was being presented under the instructions of the Japanese Government. The Ambassador replied that it was. As soon as he had finished reading the document, the Secretary turned to the Japanese Ambassador and said: 'I must say that in all my conversations with you during the last nine months, I have never uttered one word of untruth. This is borne out absolutely by the record. In all my fifty years of public service I have never seen a document that was more crowded with infamous falsehoods and distortions on a scale so huge that I never imagined until today that any government on this planet was capable of uttering them.' The Ambassador then left the room without comment.

THE JAPANESE GOVERNMENT REGRETS TO HAVE TO NOTIFY HEREBY THE AMERICAN GOVERNMENT IT CANNOT BUT CONSIDER THAT IT IS IMPOSSIBLE TO REACH AN AGREEMENT THROUGH FURTHER NEGOTIATIONS.

One week before the document was given to Secretary Hull, the following final warning message was issued to key American and British personnel by the U.S. Chief of Naval Operations: 'This dispatch is to be considered a war warning. Negotiations with Japan looking toward stabilization of conditions in the Pacific have ceased and an aggressive move by Japan is expected within the next few days. The number and equipment of Japanese troops and the organization of naval task forces indicates an amphibious expedition against either the Philippines, Thai [land], K[o]r[e]a peninsula or possibly Borneo. Execute an appropriate defensive deployment preparatory to carrying out the tasks assigned in WPL46. Inform District and Army authorities. A similar warning is being sent by War Department. Spenavo inform British.'

The Japanese task force commander, Vice Admiral Chiuchi Nagumo, received a signal from Yamamoto on 2 December which read: 'Niitaka Yama Nabora' or 'Climb Mount Niitaka', the authorization to begin the operation against Pearl. Admiral Nagumo had positioned his fleet exactly 230 miles north of the Hawaiian island of Oahu on 7 December and his carriers began launching their bomb and torpedo-laden aircraft at 6 a.m. that day. Fifty A6M2 Zeke (Zero) fighters accompanied forty Nakajima B5N2 Kate low-level torpedo-bombers, fifty high-level Kates and fifty Val dive-bombers. At 7:53 a.m. the first wave of Japanese planes passed Barber's Point and approached their target. They would be followed an hour later by a second wave of 170 bombers.

Skirting the Oahu coastline at an altitude of 9,800 feet, the raiders began their descent towards the harbour which that morning was sheltering ninety-four American warships of various types. The ships were not protected by anti-torpedo netting as the Navy did not believe they were vulnerable to attack by Japanese forces so far from Japan.

The first targets to be struck by the raiders were the Pearl Harbor Naval Air Station on Ford Island and Hickam Field, as nine dive-bombers from *Shokaku* blasted the hangars and aircraft on the Ford Island apron. Then eighteen more dive-bombers from the same carrier

left: Landing Signal Officer aboard a U.S. Navy carrier in WW2; below: An F6F Hellcat in a carrier take-off.

and dive-bombers from *Zuikaku* were busy pounding Wheeler Field, as fighters from *Soryu* and Hiryu were establishing Japanese control of the airspace over Wheeler. But the greatest airfield damage was sustained at Kaneohe Naval Air Station, where most of the station's aircraft were destroyed by planes from *Shokaku* and *Zuikaku*.

Next, lumbering torpedo-bombers from *Akagi* and *Kaga* began their run on the warships moored northwest of Ford Island, as other torpedo aircraft homed in on the vessels of Battleship Row and those at Ten-Ten Pier.

The battleships *Arizona, California, Nevada, Oklahoma* and *West Virginia* were all struck by torpedoes. A direct bomb hit down the funnel of *Arizona* caused her forward ammunition magazines to explode. She broke in two and capsized, taking the lives of more than a thousand of her crew. Many crewmen from *Tennessee* and *Maryland* died when their vessels were bombed and they tried to escape by leaping into the water which was covered with a heavy layer of burning oil. In her drydock, *Pennsylvania* was enveloped by a cloud of thick black smoke which may have protected her from greater damage. In another drydock the destroyer *Shaw* was hit and, in the most spectacular explosion of the entire attack, was blown apart, her demise captured on film in one of the most dramatic photographs of the war.

Nevada was now endeavouring to run through the carnage and make her way out of the narrow channel to the open sea. She came under a renewed attack, but was successfully beached out of harm's way. The burning, badly damaged *West Virginia* had settled onto the bottom of the harbour. Within days, *California*, the victim of three torpedo hits, would do the same. *Oklahoma* lay overturned, her masts in the mud of the bottom. *Maryland* suffered relatively minor damage; *Utah* had capsized, and *Tennessee* had taken two major bomb hits. Thirteen smaller vessels were sunk or damaged, including the destroyers *Cassin* and *Downes* in drydocks near the *Pennsylvania*.

The attack was over by 10 a.m. In addition to the many U.S. Navy ships damaged or sunk, 188 aircraft had been destroyed and five more planes from the inbound carrier *Enterprise* were shot down by mistake. In all, more than 2,400 U.S. personnel were killed in the various attacks on American military installations on Oahu that day. The Japanese lost just twenty-

above: U.S. Navy fighter pilot Edward Wendorf;
top right: Crash on deck of a Royal Navy F4F
Grumman Martlet; below: Carrier deck crews
humping a Dauntless dive-bomber into her
take-off position.

above: Morris Montgomery survived the sinking of the carrier USS *Gambier Bay*; top right: A Grumman Wildcat fighter on her carrier; below: A wounded gunner is lifted from the turret of his Avenger torpedo bomber in WW2.

nine aircraft of the 360 that participated in the raids.

In the attack, the oil tank farm facility and the dockyard installations were mostly undamaged. Of the targetted battleships, only four were actually sunk, and much of the damage done was repairable. The battleship *Nevada* later took part in the D-Day invasion of Normandy and the battle of Iwo Jima. Of the battleships at Pearl on 7 December, five were repaired and active within the next three years. The damaged airfield facilities were soon repaired.

The American aircraft carriers were unaffected by the attack and, shortly, they and their successors would become the nucleus of the new U.S. Navy striking force, the new capital ships. The primary effect of the elaborately planned and carefully executed Pearl Harbor raid was, as Admiral Yamamoto had feared, to wake a sleeping giant. Jolted from their isolationism

left: Japanese Kamikaze pilots in the final days of the war; below: The result of a Kamikaze attack on the carrier USS *Bunker Hill*.

by the shocking surprise attack, stunned and disbelieving, the American people soon rallied. They were united in their determination to avenge 'the date which will live in infamy,' as President Franklin Roosevelt referred to it in his declaration of war address to the U.S. Congress on 8 December. That same day Britain, at war with Germany since September 1939, declared war on Japan. The Pearl Harbor attack had caused the United States to enter the war and ally with Britain, initially against Japan, and then against Germany and Italy as well. By 11 December, what had been essentially a European conflict had become a world war. The Japanese armed forces controlled Manchuria, French Indochina and parts of China by 7 December when they began their new offensive in southeast Asia and the Pacific. They moved swiftly to invade the Philippines, Hong Kong, Thailand, Guam, Singapore, Malaya, British Borneo and the Dutch East Indies. They aimed to drive the British, Dutch and Americans out

F/A-18 multi-role fighters aboard a
U.S. nuclear supercarrier.

of Asia; to implement their 'co-prosperity sphere'; increase their power base and secure for themselves the natural resources they required for their effort to conquer China and, ultimately, to weaken and demoralize the United States and force her to negotiate for peace on Japan's terms.

In pursuit of these aims, the Japanese also took Burma within a year of the Pearl Harbor attack and began seizing bases and facilities in the Solomon Islands, New Guinea and the Aleutian Islands. But the key to Japan's ultimate success in the Pacific, as outlined by Admiral Yamamoto, would be Midway Island. There, the admiral believed, 'The success or failure of our entire strategy in the Pacific will be determined by . . . destroying the United States fleet, more particularly its carrier task forces . . . by launching the proposed operations against Midway, we can succeed in drawing out the enemy's carrier strength and destroying it in decisive battles.'

The Battle of Midway lasted from 3 to 6 June 1942 and was among the greatest battles of the war. In it carrier aircraft of the Japanese and American fleets clashed near the central Pacific island, with the Japanese losing 250 planes and four of their six carriers. Just as Midway was the beginning of the end for Japan in the war, so it was the beginning of the end of the battleship's reign as the principal capital ship of the world's naval powers.

Rear Admiral Chester C. Woods, Commandant of the U.S. Third Naval District, stated at the decommissioning of the USS *Wisconsin* on 8 March 1958: "We have seen the end of the trail for this magnificent breed of ship. The battleship is finally turning over her mantle of naval primacy to new and more effective weapons, a primacy which has been held by the battleship, or line-of-battle warship, for many hundreds of years of sail and a hundred years of steam. The battleship is still the heavyweight of all the ships in the world which utilize only their built-in power to inflict damage to the enemy. But when the hitting power of a ship could be extended far beyond the range of the guns of a battleship, as in the case of the carrier and its embarked aircraft, then the supremacy of the battleship was doomed. The new 'king' is the carrier. But some day it too will pass on, giving way to another king of that future era—the guided-missile ship or something else which we cannot now know."

Aircraft carriers had become the dreadnoughts of our time.

Rear Admiral Heijiro Abe, Imperial Japanese Navy (Ret), retained a souvenir of his visit to Pearl Harbor on 7 December 1941, a yellowing photograph he had taken from his Nakajima bomber as the squadron he commanded dropped their armour-piercing bombs on the vessels in Battleship Row. On his first run over the harbour, Abe encountered heavy smoke from an earlier attack by Japanese torpedo-bombers. The smoke obscured his target, the USS *West Virginia*, forcing him to lead the squadron around for a second run. When he released his single bomb he watched it strike what he believed must have been the ship's powder magazine. He recalled seeing the great ship shake convulsively and belch flames from many openings. He recorded that instant with his German-made camera and returned to his carrier where he had four prints of the photo made—one for the carrier task force chief, one for the skipper of his ship, one for Imperial Headquarters in Tokyo and one for himself. His print is the only one known to have survived the war. He has guarded the photo carefully over the years. His greatest wish has been to one day return to Pearl Harbor "to offer prayers for the repose of the fallen Americans there. I have to do it before I die."

And now I see with eye serene / The very pulse of the machine; a traveller between life and death; the reason firm, the temperate will, / Endurance, foresight, strength and skill; / A perfect woman, nobly planned; / To warn, to comfort, and command; / And yet a Spirit still, and bright / With something of angelic light.
—from *She Was a Phantom of Delight* by William Wordsworth

As her lines were cast off, and the nuclear-powered aircraft carrier USS *Harry S. Truman* and the ships of her battle group got under way on her January 2003 deployment, the following announcement was heard over the ship's public address system: (1MC) PEACE ON EARTH TO MEN OF GOOD WILL . . . ALL OTHERS—STAND BY.

In a move calculated to boost civilian morale in the United States, as well as to begin to pay the Japanese back for their raid on Pearl Harbor, the U.S. Army Air Force planned and carried out a bold bombing attack on Tokyo in spring 1942. Led by Lieutenant Colonel James Doolittle, a force of sixteen B-25 Mitchell bombers took off from the flight deck of the carrier USS *Hornet* on the morning of 18 April. They flew 550 miles west to bomb various targets in the Japanese capital city. While the damage done was relatively small, the point had been made. It was a tiny taste of the whirlwind Japan would reap before she would finally be forced to surrender in the summer of 1945.

I was born on an Irish sea of eggs and porter, / I was born in Belfast, in the MacNeice country, / A child of Harland & Wolff in the iron forest, / My childbed a steel cradle slung from a gantry.
    I remember the Queen's Road trams swarming with workers, / The lovely northern voices, the faces of the women, / The plane trees by the City Hall: an Alexander Platz, And the sailors coming off shore with silk stockings and linen.
    I remember the jokes about sabotage and Dublin, / The noisy jungle of cranes and sheerlegs, the clangour, / The draft in February of a thousand matelots from Devonport, / Surveying anxiously my enormous flight deck and hangar.
    I remember the long vista of ships under the quiet mountain, / The signals from Belfast Castle, the usual panic and sea-fever/ Before I slid superbly out on the green lough / Leaving the tiny cheering figures on the jetty for ever.
    Turning my face from home to the Southern Cross, / A map of crackling stars, and the albatross.
—HMS *Glory* by Charles Causley

top right: A Royal Navy Sea Harrier
departing HMS *Illustrious*; right: A flight
deck sailor of *Illustrious*; far right:
Homecoming for a Royal Navy aviator.

Scharnhorst and Gneisenau

Firing exercises by the German warship *Scharnhorst*.

There was a sense of urgency in the planning of Germany's next generation of pocket battleship or Panzerschiff in 1932. The new French *Dunkerque* class battleship was causing great concern among the German design staff, which held that the next Panzerschiff must be a far more powerful warship than the soon-to-be-launched *Dunkerque*. The three existing Panzerschiffs already exceeded the 10,000-ton maximum imposed on German warships by the Versailles Treaty. Now the designers no longer pretended to honour the limitation as the Germans sought to achieve a vessel superior to the French threat in one of 26,000 tons, which would grow to 38,900 tons fully loaded, by the time the two ships of the *Scharnhorst* class were completed in 1939.

By retaining high-pressure steam for their power, instead of the newer diesel technology, the creators of *Scharnhorst* and *Gneisenau* produced a warship capable of 31.5 knots. The armament consisted of nine 11-inch guns, twelve 5.9-inch guns, fourteen 4.1-inch guns and sixteen 37mm guns. Much debate surrounded the decision to go with 11-inch main guns, as larger guns were clearly desirable to counter the thirteen-inch weapons of *Dunkerque*. 11-inch guns were selected, however, with provision being made for the possible installation of larger guns at some future date. The armour belt tapered from a maximum of 13.8 inches to 6.7 inches and two-inch armour covered the upper deck surface. Although the Allies would continue to describe the two ships as battlecruisers, **the Kriegsmarine** always rated them as battleships. *Gneisenau* was completed before *Scharnhorst* and, during initial sea trials, it was found that too much water was coming aboard forward, so a new clipper or 'Atlantic' bow was added in late 1938. Repositioning the anchors further reduced excessive spray, and smoke around the bridge was reduced with the addition of a large funnel cap. Radar was installed in 1938 and augmented in 1942, and the catapult and aircraft hangar were also modified. *Scharnhorst* was given an Atlantic bow and the large funnel cap in 1939. Her first sea trial into the Atlantic came in late March 1939. *Gneisenau* and *Scharnhorst* had passed their sea trials by 22 August and, when World War Two broke out in September, both were at anchor in the River Elbe near Hamburg. In early October, *Gneisenau* sailed to the port of Wilhelmshaven. She then departed on a North Sea operation in the company of a cruiser and nine destroyers. *Scharnhorst*, meanwhile, was undergoing repairs to her superstructure, damaged during a target practice exercise.

On 21 November, *Scharnhorst* and *Gneisenau* left Wilhelmshaven to harass the British Northern Patrol, a line of cruisers stretched across the Iceland-Faeroes Gap. They were accompanied by the light cruisers *Köln* and *Leipzig* initially, but continued on their own after their second day at sea. Vizeadmiral Wilhelm Marschall was in command of the German warships. The group had not been detected by British reconnaissance aircraft or submarines and the Admiralty did not know of their presence in the area, or even that they were at sea.

On the 22nd, *Scharnhorst* claimed her first victim of the war, the 16,600-ton armed merchant cruiser HMS *Rawalpindi*, a converted passenger liner, under the command of Captain E.C. Kennedy. She mounted eight six-inch guns and two three-inch anti-aircraft guns. *Rawalpindi* was sighted by the *Scharnhorst* lookouts at 4:07 p.m. and when the *Scharnhorst* ordered her to halt, Captain Kennedy ignored the demand and immediately signalled the Commander, Home Fleet, his position and that he had sighted "the enemy battlecruiser *Deutschland*", having mistakenly identified *Scharnhorst* as such. At this point, Kennedy tried to reach the safety of a nearby fog bank, but was cut off by *Scharnhorst*, which fired a shot across the British vessel's bow. One of Kennedy's lookouts then sighted another ship in the distance, which he took to be part of the British Northern Patrol. Kennedy headed the *Rawalpindi* towards the distant vessel, seeking its support in the situation, only to discover shortly that the other ship was *Gneisenau*.

Altering course again, Kennedy prepared his ship to fight *Scharnhorst*. As he did so, Vizeadmiral Marschall ordered him to abandon ship. Kennedy responded with his six-inch guns and tried to shield his ship in smoke. The distance between the two enemies was shortening rapidly, and when it fell to less than 8,000 yards, *Scharnhorst* began firing on *Rawalpindi*. Except for Captain Kennedy, a Chief Petty Officer, and one sailor, everyone on the bridge of the British vessel was killed by the first German salvo. Now *Rawalpindi* was receiving fire from the distant *Gneisenau* as well. The German warships were scoring dramatic hits on the merchant cruiser, starting immense fires too furious to contain and disabling many of her guns and much of her power supply. Then, as Kennedy led a party of two ratings aft in an effort to put their smoking generator back into action, a shell burst nearby, killing all three of them.

Out of control and out of the fight, the flaming hulk of *Rawalpindi* began to sink. In eight minutes of firing, *Scharnhorst* and *Gneisenau* had put 141 heavy shells into and near the British vessel, and ceased their firing. *Rawalpindi* exploded at 5:30 p.m. Vizeadmiral Marschall gave the order to pick up survivors, a humane act that jeopardized his battleships which were brightly illuminated by the burning wreck of his target. At 7:14 p.m., he halted the rescue

German Chancellor Adolf Hitler, far left, at the launch of the *Scharnhorst* in 1936; below: Ice-covered in the Baltic in January 1940; right: The forward secondary 150mm turret of *Gneisenau*; bottom right: HMS *Duke of York* firing her main guns in rough seas off Scapa Flow.

SCHARNHORST Class Ch—
Forward Secondary & AA
Batt—

operation. The two German warships left the scene, carrying twenty-seven survivors from *Rawalpindi.*

After their successful raiding mission, *Scharnhorst* and *Gneisenau* sailed back to Brest for repairs. This suited the British, who made plans to keep them bottled up in the French port. Over the next several months the RAF conducted a series of air raids on the German battleships at Brest, causing considerable damage and delaying their scheduled return to their assigned duties. In their efforts to destroy *Scharnhorst* and *Gneisenau*, the RAF flew 3,599 bombing sorties to the French port. 2,692 of these sorties completed their attacks, dropping a total of 4,118 tons of bombs on the town, the harbour, and the ships. They lost fifty-three aircraft in the attacks.

On 13 November 1941, German Navy Commander-in-Chief Admiral Erich Raeder tried to persuade Hitler to agree to a series of short strikes by *Scharnhorst* and *Gneisenau* against enemy operations in the Atlantic beginning in February 1942, when the two ships would again be fully ready for sea duty. Hitler was preoccupied with events in Russia and responded by asking Raeder if he could get the two battleships back to Germany by means of a surprise dash up the English Channel. On Christmas Day the Führer decided that the continuing threat to the battleships in Brest was intolerable and that they were to be brought back to Germany and then re-deployed to Norway. Raeder and the senior German admirals opposed the idea as too risky. Finally, Hitler gave Raeder the choice of either bringing the battleships back to Germany via the Channel, or scrapping them. On 12 January 1942, Raeder accepted the high-risk option, which became known as Operation Cerberus.

The plan called for the two warships, in company with *Prinz Eugen*, to leave Brest at night and hopefully surprise the British by passing through the Dover narrows in daylight; the Germans believing that the British would expect the passage to occur in darkness. With *Scharnhorst* in the lead, the vessels, under the command of Vizeadmiral Otto Ciliax, left Brest at 10:25 p.m. on 11 February, after yet another raid on the harbour by the RAF with no appreciable result. They had slipped out of port and into open water undetected.

At high speed the three warships headed past the Somme Estuary towards the Channel narrows, under the protective cover of a Luftwaffe escort. It was then that an RAF fighter patrol spotted the German aircraft and the warships they were guarding. The patrol reported the sighting and the position. At midday, the German vessels passed Cap Gris Nez, within sight of British shore-based gun batteries, which fired on but failed to hit the warships. In the next few hours the German ships came under attack by Fleet Air Arm Swordfish biplanes out of RAF Manston in Kent, destroyers from Harwich, RAF Beauforts, and motor torpedo boats, all to no avail.

As the vessels passed north of Ostend, through the coastal shipping lanes that had been heavily mined by the Royal Air Force, *Scharnhorst* struck and detonated one of the magnetic mines, causing some damage and slowing her temporarily. But she was soon able to make twenty-five knots again. Ciliax was running his charges off the Dutch coast and the weather was deteriorating. The RAF then sent nearly 400 bomber sorties against the German warships. Only ten per cent of them even located their targets and none hit them. In the futile attacks, the RAF lost three Wellingtons, three Beauforts, nine Hampdens and two Blenheims.

The warships continued eastward and, off the island of Terschelling, both *Scharnhorst* and *Gneisenau* struck mines. *Scharnhorst* lost most of her power and shipped more than a thousand tons of water. She struggled to continue, but finally made port in Wilhelmshaven. *Gneisenau* and *Prinz Eugen* arrived safely in the River Elbe early in the morning of 13 February. The Germans had succeeded in executing their Channel Dash; Britain was embarrassed, but neither *Scharnhorst* nor *Gneisenau* would ever reach the Atlantic again.

Badly damaged in a raid on Kiel in February 1942, *Gneisenau* would see no further action in the war. She was moved to Götenhafen to be rearmed with fifteen-inch guns, but that work was halted in January 1943. On 27 March 1945, *Gneisenau* was scuttled for use as a blockship at Götenhafen, and would be broken up for scrap between 1947 and 1951.

By November 1943, Germany's war with Russia was going badly for the Reich and pressure was put on the German Navy to disrupt and destroy the Allied supply convoys to Murmansk. For the winter of 1943-44, *Scharnhorst* moved to Norway and given the tasks of countering any attempted Allied landing in Norway, Jutland or northern Finland, attacking Allied arctic convoys, mining and/or bombarding enemy routes and bases, and, by her presence, tying up enemy warships.

On 18 December 1943, the German Navy, monitoring British radio traffic, learned that a major new convoy was being readied for the run to Murmansk. It was convoy JW55B, consisting of nineteen merchant ships due to leave Loch Awe, Scotland, and on 20 December. *Scharnhorst* was made ready for sea and departed Altafiord together with five destroyers on the evening of Christmas Day. The small force under the command of Vizeadmiral Erich Bey, departed in a fearsome gale and sub-zero temperature.

Sailing with the convoy and providing protection were two British warship groups. Force One made up of the cruisers *Belfast, Sheffield,* and *Norfolk*, and Force Two, under the command of Admiral Sir Bruce Fraser, consisting of the battleship *Duke of York* and the cruiser *Jamaica*. Fraser knew, via Ultra decrypts, that the German warships were under way. The British and German forces were sailing into a force eight gale, in extremely heavy seas. The weather was worsening, with increasing sleet and snow. Through the night both forces continued towards Bear Island and in the early morning of the 26th, *Scharnhorst*"s destroyer escort spread out in search of the convoy. The two enemy forces approached each other, and a radar operator in *Belfast* had the first contact with *Scharnhorst* at 8:40 a.m. The battleship was then just thirty miles south of the convoy and closing rapidly.

At 9:30 a.m. *Norfolk* opened fire, landing two shells on *Scharnhorst* and destroying her main radar. Vizeadmiral Bey ordered the battleship on a new course to the south, easily outdistancing the British cruisers giving chase. After twenty-five minutes, Bey again changed course, heading *Scharnhorst* northeast towards the convoy. The British cruisers also altered course in order to position themselves between *Scharnhorst* and the convoy they were shepherding. They had lost radar contact with the German battleship, but by noon, *Belfast* regained it. In a few moments, the enemies were in sight of each other and Bey again tried to take *Scharnhorst* away from a new confrontation with the cruisers which pursued her. Sporadic gunfire was soon being exchanged and in the action, *Norfolk* lost her radar and one of her turrets. Both *Scharnhorst* and *Sheffield* received hits but only minor damage resulted.

below: *Gneisenau*, sister ship of *Scharnhorst*; right: *Scharnhorst* at sea after her 1939 refit.

Now, Bey cut off the exchange and turned *Scharnhorst* away and back at high speed towards the safety of Altafiord. He could not know that Admiral Fraser was bringing British Force Two in the direction of the fiord to cut off the German battleship.

It was late afternoon and quite dark when the two capital ships came within sight of each other. In an early exchange of fire, one of the forward turrets of *Scharnhorst* was put out of action, but the other gunners of the German battleship were soon able to straddle *Duke of York* with their shells. Then the British battleship replied with several shots that landed on *Scharnhorst*. A hit pierced her armour belt and exploded in the number one boiler room, causing a partial loss of power to her main turbines. *Scharnhorst* was no longer able to summon the great speed that had enabled her to outrun her adversaries. The range between her and the enemy warships began to shrink. The great German warship was now prey to both British forces which were closing on her. She was soon struck by four torpedoes, on both sides of her hull. All of the British warships pressed their attacks on the German battleship and she received a total of fourteen torpedoes in the action. Fires raged in her, lighting up the arctic night. Her ordeal finally ended when horrific flashes signalled the explosions of her ammunition magazines at 7:45 p.m.

The future Royal Navy Admiral of the Fleet Sir Henry Leach was a young Sub-Lieutenant assigned to the spotting plot in the fourteen-inch gun transmitting station of HMS *Duke of York*. He recalled the action against Scharnhorst: "Such was the strength of the Germans, based off Norway, and such was there ability to interfere with Russian convoys, that the convoys were ceased. The game simply wasn't worth the candle because the losses were too great, particularly during the summer months. In those waters in winter it's always dark and in summer it's always light. In winter you got a sort of twilight between about midday and

three in the afternoon; in summer you didn't get any twilight at all. The Russians squealed a bit about stopping the convoys, of course, and it was decided, partly to pacify the Russians and partly to draw out the *Scharnhorst* which posed a great threat to the convoys, to restart the convoys but under a heavy, heavy escort.

"The *Belfast* and other ships were covering a southbound convoy, and the *Duke of York* and the *Jamaica*, a six-inch cruiser, were standing in the deep field, broadly covering three convoys. It was around Christmas Eve 1943. A signal came from Admiral Burnett, who was commanding the second cruiser squadron in the *Belfast*, that the southbound convoy had been attacked by the *Scharnhorst*.

"The weather was absolutely foul. *Scharnhorst* had made a pass at that convoy, and was beaten off by the *Belfast* and another cruiser, so at least we knew then that the *Scharnhorst* had left her shelter and was at sea. Now, Bruce Fraser in the *Duke of York*, the C-in-C, had to decide what the German battleship would do. Would she try to break out into the Atlantic as the *Bismarck* had done, or would she, once the convoy had passed and she had done little damage to it, return to her Norwegian base? In fact, *Scharnhorst* made a second attack on the southbound convoy and was again beaten off. Bruce Fraser guessed that, under the weather conditions at the time, she would probably return to base in Norway and he set course accordingly.

"On Christmas Day we increased speed, so far as we could in the weather at the time. The *King George V* class were 'wet ships'. They had a fairly low freeboard and going into a heavy sea, they kicked it right up, and the forward turret was virtually under water. They were fine ships, but they were wet.

"In the evening of Christmas Day, we went to action stations. The policy in those days, and it was a very sensible one, was that you went to action stations when it got dark, if you were in a particular threat area, and all hands slept—in so far as they could—at their action stations. Because it was the very early days of radar and it was not at all reliable, this meant that if you got jumped in the middle of the night, instead of the inevitable confusion of going to action stations once the enemy had been detected, you were there already and all you had to do was roll over and do your stuff. So, everybody went to action stations and then the not inconsiderable problem was, how do you feed them? In those days, you had individual messing as opposed to cafeteria messing, which didn't come for decades after that. The quality of food was pretty dreadful because they had to cart it long distances in unheated containers, so it was cold and greasy and generally pretty unpleasant. And in those weather conditions everybody was feeling seasick anyway because even a ship that size was bucketing around.

"It wasn't until late afternoon of the day after Christmas when word was broadcast that the *Scharnhorst* had been driven off from the convoy and was last detected steaming south, more or less straight towards us.

"We were all cold and hungry and tired, but everybody wanted to get into this action and clobber the enemy. Fraser's plan was that, unless the enemy opened fire first, we would hold our fire until the range was 12,000 yards, because radar was uncertain and so was night action; you depended on star shells for illuminating the target. Sitting there in my rather wet suit in the forward part of A turret, I could watch the range counter ticking down until it showed 12,000 yards, and at 12,000 yards the five-two-fives opened fire with star shells and the fourteen-inch also opened up. And when the star shells burst on the far side of the *Scharnhorst*, she was jumped. She simply didn't know that we were there. She was heading straight for us. Her turrets were trained fore and aft and she wasn't ready.

"As soon as the star shell burst, she turned away. She was capable of greater speed than the *Duke of York* and she turned, really, to make her base back in Norway. We altered course to follow her. The weather conditions were truly foul. We fired a number of salvoes, but as the distance between us increased to 20,000 yards or so, our firing was checked. I can't tell you how galling that was, that after all this effort, and having caught her with her trousers down, she was going to escape into the night. And there was nothing we could do about it. The destroyers were dispatched to carry out a torpedo attack, but again, under those weather conditions, they could hardly go faster than the *Duke of York*.

"Then, quite suddenly, I think around eight o'clock, the change of range ceased and the range counters started to click down again. The range was closing. This, I think, was due to a hit. *Scharnhorst* had had to reduce speed, enabling the destroyers and the *Duke of York* to catch up, and we opened fire again as soon as we got within effective range. Then the end came quite quickly. The destroyers scored torpedo hits. We closed right in to something like 2,000 yards and it was a dreadful sight. *Scharnhorst* was on fire from end to end. People were silhouetted against the fire, jumping over the side into the water. It was reckoned that if you were in that cold water for more than three minutes, you didn't survive. And then she sank, and that was that.

"We were all very tired and I can remember feeling 'thank God that's over and we won, she's gone . . . it was success and we had achieved a mega-victory, but tempered by a sadness that a very fine ship had gone to the bottom. I think that there were about thirty-three survivors who were picked up by the destroyers and transferred to us."

Scharnhorst sank, taking 1,803 of her crew with her and ending the Battle of the North Cape. Of Germany's great battleships, only *Tirpitz* remained.

Twenty-year-old Pat Kingsmill was flying one of six Swordfish torpedo-bombers attacking the German battlecruisers *Scharnhorst* and *Gneisenau* and the heavy cruiser *Prinz Eugen* off Calais on 21 February 1941. Kingsmill and the other members of Fleet Air Arm Squadron 825 had had no combat experience before this assignment. As the elderly biplanes of the squadron approached the German warships at ninety knots, Kingsmill was following his leader, Lt. Cdr. Eugene Esmonde, when the latter was shot down as the flight neared the target ships. Then a second Swordfish became a fireball as Kingsmill watched. At a distance of 2,000 yards from his target, the *Prinz Eugen*, he banked onto a direct line to the vessel and received a bullet wound in the back. Flying on through heavy smoke and shell bursts, Kingsmill's observer was wounded in the leg and his telegraphist-gunner had to straddle a huge hole in the fuselage to keep from falling into the sea. Now the aircraft was hit again, starting a fire on one wing and damaging the engine. The pilot had to struggle with the controls which were becoming more and more sluggish as he tried circling to evade harassing enemy fighters. He attempted to align on the *Prinz Eugen* to drop his torpedo, but the German warship manoeuvred violently and Kingsmill's torpedo narrowly missed astern of the vessel. The Swordfish was then hit again, its wings severely damaged. Kingsmill fought to keep the plane from stalling before he could ditch it in the sea. That accomplished, the pilot crawled back along the fuselage and assisted his crew from the sinking aircraft. Their small dinghy had been damaged by the gunfire and was useless. But, within ten minutes they were rescued by an RAF torpedo boat. All of the 825 Squadron Swordfish were shot down that day. For his part in the action, Kingsmill was awarded the Distinguished Service Order.

At 4p.m. on 8 June 1940, lookouts on the German battleship *Scharnhorst* sighted the British aircraft carrier HMS *Glorious*, which was being escorted off Norway by two Royal Navy destroyers. *Glorious* had no air reconnaissance patrols airborne at the time and she was caught by surprise when the enemy battleships arrived. Gunners of *Scharnhorst* began firing at *Glorious* at 4:32 p.m. from a distance of 28,500 yards. Six minutes later a shell from the battleship struck *Glorious*, starting a large fire on the flight deck. At 4:42 p.m., the sister ship of *Scharnhorst*, *Gneisenau*, opened fire. One of her shells hit the carrier's bridge, killing the captain and most of the personnel there. At 4:56 a smokescreen from the escorting British destroyers caused the two German battleships to cease firing. One of the destroyers, HMS *Ardent*, then launched a series of eight torpedoes but made no hits on the German warships, which then began firing on *Ardent*. They quickly sank the destroyer. The battleships then resumed firing on *Glorious* and hit her in the centre engine room. At 5:30 the destroyer HMS *Acasta* launched a torpedo which struck *Scharnhorst*, tearing a massive hole in her hull and causing her to take in 2,500 tons of seawater. Her after main gun turret was put out of action as well, and forty-eight of her crew were killed. The British aircraft carrier was severely damaged in the continuing attack and at 6:10 p.m., she capsized and sank. Ten minutes later the same fate befell *Acasta*. More than 1,500 Royal Navy sailors died in this action.

Fast and Last

The USS *Wisconsin* at the Hampton Roads Naval Museum, Norfolk, Virginia.

The four fast battleships of the *Iowa* class are the world's last battleships. They are BB61, the USS *Iowa*, BB62, the USS *New Jersey*, BB63, the USS *Missouri*, and BB64, the USS *Wisconsin*. The last of the last is the *Missouri*. While construction of *Wisconsin* began later than that of *Missouri*, and she had a higher hull number, *Missouri* was, in fact, the world's last battleship to be completed, serve and survive.

The idea behind the "fast battleship" stems from a desire among the great naval powers to combine the best characteristics of their battleships and their battle cruisers in order to develop a warship with great speed, firepower and armoured protection. In general, battle cruisers had been faster than battleships, but had lighter armour protection and thus greater vulnerability to enemy attack. As major improvements in gun calibre, ballistic efficiency and fire control increased the fighting range of the battleship, the battle cruiser's speed advantage over her big sister was nullified.

Near the end of the 1920s, the U.S. Navy and the U.S. Bureau of Construction and Repair were involved in design studies for a new battleship. They avidly followed the progress of the new British *Rodney* class battleships, *Rodney* and *Nelson*, which were expected to establish a new standard for capital ships to come.

Following the end of the First World War, developing trade interests in the Pacific caused the United States to concentrate much of her warship fleet on the U.S. west coast for the protection of those interests and American possessions. By 1935, it was clear to U.S. naval strategists that the nation's next war would be with Japan. Japanese naval planners, meanwhile, were bridling under the terms of the 1922 Washington Naval Treaty, which they perceived as a conspiracy to confine them to the role of a secondary naval power. They reacted by starting a major programme of warship modernization and radical reconstruction to develop the most formidable naval fighting force possible. One example of that effort was the refitting 1911-1913 *Kongo* class battle cruisers, which they twice modified on a large scale to recreate them as full-fledged battleships capable of 30.5 knots.

By the mid-1930s, U.S. intelligence was indicating that Japan was focused on developing an entirely new class of super battleship, posing an unacceptable level of threat to America's interests and her navy. In 1935, an intensive effort led to development and approval of designs for the new *North Carolina* class, a 37,000-ton battleship armed with nine sixteen-inch guns in three turrets and capable of a 28-knot speed. In armament she was comparable to the *Rodney* class battleships of the Royal Navy. But *North Carolina* had been planned with fourteen-inch guns and, when she was later up-rated to larger main weapons, the U.S. Chief of Naval Operations argued that her original armour left her under-protected and he opposed an allocation for two further *North Carolina* class warships in 1937.

Instead, another new class of battleship was introduced that year. The *South Dakota* class featured a clever re-arrangement of the main spaces for machinery, operational plotting and ammunition magazines, in a shorter hull, together with a new armour layout, allowing considerable weight savings. These improvements on the *North Carolina* design, coupled with an additional 9,000 shaft horsepower, resulted in a highly successful, better protected battleship of roughly the same performance characteristics as the *North Carolinas*. Many aspects of the *South Dakota* design, in particular the approach to armour protection, were to be highly influential in the final fast battleship class.

The London Naval Conference of 1935, from which the Japanese had formally withdrawn,

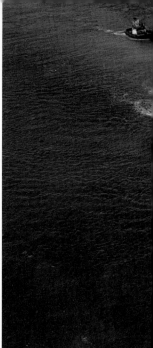

marked the point when they fully implemented *Yamato,* the battleship construction pro-gramme they had been planning since 1930. This fantastic new class capital ship would dwarf all existing, building, and planned battleships. At 69,500 tons, *Yamato* was to be armed with nine eighteen-inch guns and was capable of 27-knots. The Japanese intended building seven of these giants—by far the largest and most powerful capital ships ever conceived and real-ized. Of the seven planned, four *Yamato* class vessels were laid down and, of these, two were actually completed—*Yamato* and *Musashi.* The Yamato programme proceeded at high-prior-ity pace, and under the strictest security precautions. The vessels themselves were shielded from observation by enormous tarpaulins, and what little the U.S. Navy knew about *Yamato* was based largely on speculation. Accurate reports on characteristics and progress of the Japanese super ship, from spies, diplomatic attachés, and analysis of Japanese radio traffic, were minimal. But American Navy speculation about *Yamato* was correct, though not actu-ally proven so until the end of World War Two.

It would seem that members of the U.S. General Board and the Secretary of the Navy did not have access to any significant intelligence about the tonnage, gun calibre or capabili-ties of *Yamato* in 1938, or did not believe the reports they did receive. Their evaluation of "slow" and "fast" battleship studies did not result in a recommendation for a design that would achieve parity with what the U.S. Navy believed *Yamato* to be.

In October 1937 a special board was established to advise the U.S. Secretary of the Navy on the design, armament and construction of new battleships. Its analysis of the fast battle-ship studies caused the members to conclude that a new capital ship of 45,000 tons with a speed of 33 knots was feasible based on the *South Dakota* design. After various parallel stud-ies were completed, the Bureau of Construction and Repair developed final requirements for the new American fast battleship and on 2 June 1938 submitted the preliminary design for a vessel designated hull number BB61, the first ship of the *Iowa* class.

The four sister ships of the new class would each be armed with nine sixteen-inch guns able to fire a 2,700-pound armour-piercing projectile 42,500 yards. Each *Iowa* class battleship would be 887 feet long with a beam of 108 feet and a draught of thirty-six feet. Eight Babcock & Wilcox boilers powered four General Electric turbine shafts which could make a speed of 32.5 knots. The standard displacement was 48,110 tons; fully loaded it was 57,540 tons. In addition to their main guns, the *Iowa* battleships went to war initially with twenty five-inch guns, eighty 40mm guns, forty-nine 20mm guns (except for the USS *Iowa*, which carried sixty 40mm and sixty 20mm guns) and three spotter aircraft. The initial crew complement was 1,921.

In the treaty resulting from a 1936 London naval arms limitation conference, the attending nations had agreed an "escalator clause" which would raise the imposed limit on capital ship gun calibre, and on displacement from 35,000 to 45,000 tons. The clause could be invoked by any of the naval powers attending, to match an increase by any non-participating nation. The United States had first invoked the escalator clause in mid-1937, increasing the gun calibre for future battleship construction to sixteen inches, to counter the Japanese. In 1938, the United States, Britain and France agreed to invoke the clause to raise the tonnage limit to 45,000, sparked by rumours and their limited information about Japanese battleship projects. Immediately thereafter, intensive design activity of the U.S. Navy's *Iowa* class of battleships began.

Three *Iowa* class vessels were planned initially, and a fourth was added to provide a back-up battleship which was to be deployed when any one of the other three Iowa ships was unavailable for duty. The fourth *Iowa* type could also be used in the Atlantic, should it be required there. Funding for two further *Iowa* class battleships was included in the 1940 U.S. budget passed by the Congress. They were to be BB65, the USS *Illinois*, and BB66, the USS *Kentucky*. Ultimately, the *Illinois* would be cancelled in 1945. *Kentucky* was launched and went through several redesigns in the 1940s and 1950s to convert her into a missile-launching battleship, and was finally scrapped in 1958.

The *Iowa*s served through much of the final two years of the war in the Pacific as part of the Fast-Carrier Task Forces. When they were first deployed their primary assignments included chasing and engaging commerce raiders, acting as commerce raiders themselves, engaging the Japanese *Kongo* class battlecruisers, and leading special strike forces.

On 27 August 1943, the *Iowa* was sent to Argentia Bay, Newfoundland, to guard against the eventual breakout of the German battleship *Tirpitz*. She then carried President Roosevelt to Cairo and Tehran for war conferences with Prime Minister Churchill and Premier Stalin. On 2 January 1944, she sailed to the Pacific as flagship of Battleship Division 7 in the Marshall Islands campaign. At the end of January she screened the aircraft carriers of Task Force 58 in air strikes on Kwajalein, Truk and Eniwetok Islands. In February she supported carrier air strikes against Saipan, Tinian, Guam and Rota. Then, on 18 March, while bombarding Mili Atoll in the Marshall Islands, she was struck by two Japanese shells, sustaining only minor damage. In April she operated in support of U.S. landings at Hollandia in New Guinea, followed by another screening of a carrier strike at Truk.

On 1 May, the *Iowa* bombarded the island of Ponape in the Carolines and on 13-14 June, she was sent to bombard Saipan and Tinian in the Marianas, going on to take part in the Battle of the Philippine Sea. In August, while part of Task Group 38, *Iowa* took part in strikes against Iwo Jima and Chichijima, followed by landings at Peleliu in September.

Still with TG38 on 10 October, *Iowa* supported carrier air strikes on Formosa and the Ryuku Islands; she then went on to support strikes against Luzon in preparation for the Leyte Gulf landings on 20 October. The namesake of her warship class then returned to San Francisco for a refit, remaining there until March 1945.

On 15 April, *Iowa* arrived in the Okinawa area where she participated in screening the fast carriers in their support of U.S. Army operations on the island. The U.S. forces were approaching the Japanese home islands at this point, and the *Iowa* was needed to cover carrier strikes against the southern mainland island of Kyushu between 25 May and 13 June. Thereafter, until the end of the war two months later, *Iowa* was engaged in the bombardment of Hitachi, Hokkaido and Muroran. She was present in Tokyo Bay on 2 September for the official surrender ceremony which took place on her sister ship, the USS *Missouri*.

The second battleship of the *Iowa* class was launched exactly one year after the Japanese attack on Pearl Harbor. The USS *New Jersey* went to war in January 1944, meeting her sister ship, USS *Iowa*, as part of Battleship Division 7 on 22 January. Her initial action came in a screening operation with Task Group 58 as the carriers *Bunker Hill*, *Cowpens* and *Monterey* launched air strikes against Eniwetok and Kwajalein. BB62 was serving as flagship of Task Group 50 on 17-18 February, when her crew first fired her main guns at the enemy, engaging two Japanese destroyers and two other vessels. She sank a trawler that day. *New Jersey* remained with TG50 until April, participating in the bombardment of Mili and covering air strikes against the Palau Islands. She covered the landings at Hollandia in April and joined six other American battleships bombarding Ponape that month. In June, *New Jersey* took part in the bombardment of Saipan and Tinian. She sailed into Pearl Harbor on 9 August, where she became flagship of the U.S. 3rd Fleet. She then went to Ulithi, operating from that Pacific fleet anchorage. For nearly a month from 28 August, *New Jersey* worked, covering air strikes against islands in the Philippines. During the battle for Leyte, she operated with a carrier group and joined TG38 in December in attacks on the island of Luzon. She spent the next month screening carrier air strikes against targets in Indo-China, Formosa, Luzon and Okinawa, and operated in the attacks on Iwo Jima from February through April and supported the landings on Okinawa. By early May *New Jersey* was back in the States at Puget Sound Navy Yard for refit, which was completed at the end of June. She bombarded Wake Island on her way back to the western Pacific, arriving at Guam on 9 August and became flagship of the U.S. 5th Fleet as the war ended.

Seaman First Class Tony Iacono: "I was on the *New Jersey* from 1943, before its commissioning, until 1946. I left it in Tokyo Bay when we were part of the occupation forces. Three years on one ship. We travelled to most of the Japanese-held islands during the war and we took them all back, one by one. We were going into the Philippine Sea in June 1944. The whole fleet had gotten through the San Bernardino Straits in the dead of night, undetected. Then we ran into a huge typhoon which we were in for six days and nights. We were going down to Hollandia to cover some operation, and when we got down there the Japanese started dropping high-altitude flares on us. You could literally read a newspaper on the deck at midnight. That's how bright it was.

"When we came back through the Philippine Sea, the Japanese were waiting for us with their Kamikazes, getting ready to sink us, which they couldn't do. We were shooting 20s and 40s and five-inch rounds at them. Then we got into the second Battle of the Philippine Sea, the Marianas Turkeyshoot. After that, the Japanese Navy wasn't worth a nickel. They were devastated.

"The *New Jersey* was never hit by enemy fire. We might have got some shrapnel on the deck, but we never took an enemy hit of any sort. We did take a hit from one of our own ships. We were in port, in Palau, I think. It was a late Sunday afternoon and the guys were watching a movie on the fantail. The ships were coming in from target practice, shooting at sleeves. Some guy was on the first deck under the main deck and a projectile came right through the deck and he was killed instantly. That was the only casualty we had on that ship while I was on it.

"It was near the end. We still had Iwo Jima and Okinawa to go, and Okinawa was holy hell. We pounded that island for a week . . . all the wagons . . . the *Iowa*, the *New Jersey*, the *Wisconsin*, the *Missouri*, the *North Dakota*, the *Washington*. We went around that island around the clock, seven days. Every five minutes there was a beep and a salvo, then, when we put troops on the shore there, all hell broke loose. The Japanese weren't about to give up that island without one helluva fight. And the Kamikazes came out in full bloom. Every time we saw a little hole in the cloud, a plane would come out of it, straight down. That first day, we saved the *Bunker Hill* from Kamikazes three times. Then the Navy Department finally said, 'You can't keep up with the fleet. You're gonna have to go back.' They sent us back to Pearl with a cruiser and two destroyers, and then on to Bremerton. And there was the *Bunker Hill*, looking like a can-opener had hit it. It had taken several hits after we left Okinawa. A ferocious battle. The Navy took more casualties there than anybody."

In the preface to his illustrated history, *Battleship New Jersey*, Commander Paul Stillwell,

A broadside fired by the USS *Missouri*.

USNR, wrote: "To go to sea in the USS *New Jersey* . . . is to have the sense that she has managed to transcend the normal limitations of time. This feeling probably becomes most evident at night as she glides through the dark sea, the water making a swishing sound as it travels from bow to stern and leaves a luminescent wake beneath the starlit sky. With the coming of night, the eyes no longer focus on the details which command attention during daytime. Instead, the imagination conjures up thousands of nights past when this majestic giant has also moved beneath these same stars. The darkness obscures the changes which have been wrought in order to make her again a potent weapon, as she was when she first took to the sea two generations ago . . . During the nocturnal walk about the forecastle comes the realization that there is much more to the ship than steel, guns and missiles. Hundreds of Navy men breathe life and purpose into her inanimate elements. It is they who give her a soul and they who inherit the legacy from thousands of *New Jersey* men who have gone before."

The *Wisconsin* reached the Pacific Fleet at Ulithi on 9 December 1944 following a successful work-up in the Caribbean that summer. As part of the 3rd Fleet, BB64 participated in the attacks on Luzon in the Philippines in late December and then covered the fast carrier strikes on the Pescadores and Formosa. Operating with the 5th Fleet in February 1945, *Wisconsin* bombarded targets near Tokyo on the 16th, sailing from there to Iwo Jima to help in the bombardment prior to the landings on the 19th. From Iwo she then went on to the Japanese main island of Honshu to attack targets there. She took part in the Okinawa campaign with TF58 and then struck at targets near Kobe and Kure, before returning to continue a bombardment of Okinawa which lasted into May. She returned to Leyte for repairs and replenishment on 18 June, after which her final assignment of the war took her back to the Japanese home islands in support of further carrier air strikes which continued until the end of the conflict in mid-August.

The last of the breed of fighting ships, the battleship *Missouri,* spent the second half of 1944 in the Atlantic working up in her sea trials. Nineteen-year-old Margaret Truman, daughter of the then United States Vice President Harry S. Truman, who was from Missouri, had broken the traditional champagne bottle over the bow of BB63 at the launching ceremony on 29 January. The *Missouri* became the fleet flagship of Vice Admiral Marc Mitscher at San Francisco and sailed to the western Pacific fleet anchorage at Ulithi in the Carolines, arriving there on 13 January 1945. Her first war assignment was as a part of Mitscher's Fast Carrier Task Force 58 in strikes against Tokyo and Yokohama on 16 and 17 February respectively. She then supported the landings on Iwo Jima, returning to Ulithi before sailing to participate in a strike on the Japanese island of Kyushu on 18 March. She joined other American battleships in bombarding Okinawa on 24 March and continued in support of U.S. action there into May. On 7 April, *Missouri* was part of a carrier group that attacked and sank Japan's *Yamato*, the largest battleship ever built.

Eighteen-year-old Seaman First Class Anthony Alessandro of Cincinnati, Ohio, had been a crew member of the USS *Missouri* for just two months when the Japanese surrender was signed on his ship. "*Missouri* sailed within a mile or two of three fleet aircraft carriers, along with destroyers and destroyer escorts. The ship's mission was to guard the fast carriers with plenty of anti-aircraft fire. Some of our fire missions were broadcast to the public back home. This action was announced throughout the *Missouri* over the 1MC loudspeaker system.

"I was practicing being a first loader on a 40mm quad anti-aircraft gun. I remember thinking that I was really exposed up there by myself. If you have a misfire, you put a bag of sand over the gun breach. I am just a little guy and I didn't know if I could even lift the bag. Every time I put in a four-round clip I prayed, 'God, please don't misfire.'

"There were times when I was so tired, I didn't care what happened. We were out at sea for more than six months at a time and during one ten-month period we traveled over 100,000 nautical miles. We were in an Okinawa typhoon with seventy-foot seas. I went out to the deck to take a look and all I saw was water above the mast. One of our kids was washed away and there was only one chance for a destroyer behind us to pick him up. Somehow, they got him and in a few days he was back on board with us. We lost two or three destroyers in that storm."

It was during this period, on 11 April, that BB63 suffered a hit by a Kamikaze Zeke aircraft which struck her starboard side at just below main deck level and abreast of her number three turret. Tony Alessandro: "He was wave-skimming and we hit that plane with everything we had. I don't know how he got through all of that flak." It was mid-afternoon when the Japanese pilot guided his fighter into the *Missouri*'s flank, killing himself and starting a fire that was soon extinguished. No *Missouri* crew members were killed and damage to the ship was relatively minor. The ship's chaplain held a brief funeral service for the Japanese pilot the following day. Some of the crew wanted no part of the ceremony for the enemy. Less than a week later, the ship was again subjected to attack by a number of Kamikaze aircraft. One of them bore in on the battleship with great tenacity as his fighter was being riddled by anti-aircraft fire from *Missouri*. He managed to clip some machinery on the fantail of the big warship before plummeting into the sea in her wake. On impact his aircraft blew apart, sending bits of metal into the ship and wounding two sailors.

On 18 May the *Missouri* was made flagship, U.S. 3rd Fleet and headquarters of Admiral William F. Halsey, Jr. At the end of the month she was busy again with TF38, screening carrier air strikes against Okinawa and later against Kyushu. After a brief stay in Leyte, she returned to Japanese home waters where she continued participation in carrier action and shore bombardment through the remainder of the war.

On 15 August, in the Oval Office of the White House in Washington DC, President Harry S. Truman, surrounded by members of the press corps., stated: "I have just received a note from the Japanese government in reply to the message forwarded to that government by the Secretary of State on August 11. I deem this reply a full acceptance of the Potsdam Declaration, which specified the unconditional surrender of Japan."

The *Missouri* was selected as the site of the official surrender signing ceremony held shortly after 9 a.m. on 2 September. In a brief address, General Douglas MacArthur stated: "We are gathered here, representatives of the major warring powers, to conclude a solemn agreement whereby peace may be restored. The issues, involving divergent ideas and ideologies, have been determined on the battlefields and hence are not for our discussion or our debate. It is my earnest hope and indeed the hope of all mankind that from this solemn occasion a better world shall emerge out of the blood and carnage of the past . . ." At the end of the ceremony General MacArthur said: "Let us pray that peace be now restored to the

above: The Japanese delegation at the surrender signing ceremonies on board the USS Missouri; below: A sixteen-inch shell from the warship.

U.S.S. MISSOURI

OVER THIS SPOT
ON 2 SEPTEMBER 1945
THE INSTRUMENT
OF FORMAL SURRENDER
OF JAPAN TO THE ALLIED POWERS
WAS SIGNED
THUS BRINGING TO A CLOSE
THE SECOND WORLD WAR

THE SHIP AT THAT TIME
WAS AT ANCHOR
IN TOKYO BAY

LATITUDE 35° 21' 17" NORTH ~ LONGITUDE 139° 45' 36" EAST

centre left: The commemorative surrender plaque in the deck of the *Missouri*; left: An RPV drone on Missouri; above: General Douglas MacArthur signing the surrender documents on 2 September 1945.

above: The breech of a sixteen-inch gun of the Japanese battleship *Nagato*; right: Gun maintenance on an *Iowa* class BB.

world and that God will preserve it always. These proceedings are closed."

MacArthur used five different pens when he signed the surrender document. The pens were later presented to U.S. Army Lieutenant General Jonathan Wainwright, Theatre Commander at Corregidor and a survivor of the Bataan Death March, British Army Lieutenant-General Arthur Percival, Commander of Malaya, the United States National Archives, the U.S. Military Academy, West Point, and Mrs Douglas MacArthur. The signing was to take place at a fine old mahogany table provided by the crew of the British battleship HMS *King George V*. However, the table was too small for the surrender documents, so an ordinary table from the enlisted men's mess of *Missouri* was substituted. It was covered with a green felt cloth from the officers' mess. It is now part of the collections of the Navy Museum at the U.S. Naval Academy, Annapolis, Maryland.

Tony Alessandro: "On 15 August 1945, news broke that the war was over. Everyone was blowing whistles and there was a lot of dancing and hugging going on—but the celebration eventually subsided. It was business as usual for the crew. Many of us were still apprehensive, and for good reason; five Japanese pilots had attacked the fleet that morning. All five were shot down by navy gunners. By 28 August the *Missouri* was headed for Tokyo Bay. A lot of my buddies and I were pretty scared. We didn't know if it was a trap or if Japan really meant

to surrender. I was on a working party with two other shipmates. We brought Japanese harbour pilots aboard from another ship while we were under way, before entering Tokyo Bay. They told us about the mine fields and harbour defences and on the morning of 29 August we passed into Tokyo Bay at Condition Two, a state of medium alert, and dropped anchor without incident.

"At 7 a.m. on 2 September, 170 newsmen and cameramen boarded *Missouri* from the destroyer *Buchanon*, to cover the surrender ceremony. In the next hour high-ranking military officials of all the Allied powers were received on board. Fleet Admiral Nimitz came on board shortly after 8:00 a.m. General of the Army Douglas MacArthur, Supreme Commander of the Allied Powers, came on board at 8:43. The eleven Japanese representatives headed by Foreign Minister Shigemitsu boarded at 8:56. I was looking down on the ceremony from the fifth deck. At 9:02 General MacArthur stepped to the battery of microphones and the twenty-three minute ceremony was broadcast to the waiting world. Ten Allied and two Japanese officials signed the surrender document and by 9:38, the Japanese emissaries had departed the ship."

The USS *Missouri* left Norfolk, Virginia, on 7 June 1954 as flagship of the Midshipman Training

"Broadway", the
main corridor in the
battleship *Missouri*.

Cruise to Lisbon, Portugal and Cherbourg, France. About one day out, the *Missouri* was joined at sea by the USS *Iowa*, the USS *New Jersey*, and the USS *Wisconsin*. The four vessels operated together for just a few hours, the first and only time the four greatest battleships of the United States Navy sailed together in the same task force.

Five feet tall and 115 pounds, Jack Delaney was just seventeen years old when he joined the crew of the *Missouri* in 1952 for her second deployment of the Korean War. He was assigned to Damage Control. "It's hard to believe it is more than fifty years since I served aboard the 'Mighty Mo.' Leaving my childhood orphanage in upstate New York behind, I reported aboard the *Missouri* with both excitement and apprehension about the adventure that lay ahead. Until then, my worldly travels were limited to the Great Lakes Naval Training Center, Illinois. The news was dominated by the Korean War and the ship was headed for action off the Korean coast.

"I was assigned to the Engineering Department, R Division. We were responsible for fire-fighting and damage control, and most importantly, for maintaining the watertight integrity of the vessel. I soon became familiar with the layout of the ship, and was astonished at how many compartments a ship of that size contained. My duties required me to go into areas of the ship that most crew members never saw, from the Admiral's cabin to the shaft alleys, and fore and aft through 'Broadway,' the longest passage on the ship. My boss was a First Class Petty Officer of fifteen years service, a tough man to work for, but easy to get along with if you did your job properly.

"We departed Norfolk in September 1952, transitting from the Atlantic to the Pacific via the Panama Canal. We shoe-horned through the locks, requiring fenders along the sides of the ship to prevent damage to both the ship and the locks. What a tight squeeze! On the way to Korea, we relieved the USS *Iowa*, off Yokosuka. It was a stunning sight, the two powerful battleships lashed together from a single buoy in Tokyo Bay."

Missouri cruised up and down the Korean coast, shelling vital targets in support of Allied troops. Delaney: "For the next six months, the days alternated between the excitement of hours at General Quarters, and the tedium of consecutive Mid-watches. The memory of spending half the night on those watches still makes me shudder. My watch had me taking soundings of the voids, to check the watertight integrity of the hull. It meant roaming throughout the ship at all hours of the day and night, For a ship with a crew of 3,000 men, it was surprisingly quiet. I often had the eerie feeling that I was completely alone on board. With only red lights to illuminate her, the ship was almost entirely dark. In such subtle light, even crowded compartments full of sleeping men can appear empty."

Another *Missouri* veteran of that Korean War second deployment is Maynard Loy, a former Gunner's Mate: "We were either at General Quarters or standing watch most of our stay off Korea. Mail call was once, maybe twice, a month, when we would refuel or take on supplies from another vessel. On 22 December 1952, a most saddening event occurred. We lost our helicopter pilot, Ensign Robert Mayhew and his two observers First Lieutenant Robert Dern and First Lieutenant Rex Ellison, USMC., while they were on a spotting mission. And, on our way back to the States, while approaching Sasebo Harbor, Japan, our captain, Warner Edsall, died on the bridge of a heart attack.

"One morning, while in Wonsan Harbor doing routine shore bombardment, the *Missouri* came under counter fire from enemy shore batteries. All three of our sixteen-inch gun turrets trained to our port side and fired a nine-gun salvo on broadside. This was a very rare occurrence as it put so much strain on the ship's superstructure, but we got the job done and pushed the enemy back so our ground forces could advance."

Herb Fahr boarded the *Missouri* for the first time in March 1954: "I got to Pier 7 at the Norfolk Navy Base and reported aboard the Mo to the Officer of the Deck in the time-honoured tradition of the Blue Jacket's Manual. First, salute the stern of the ship, where the American flag is flown when the ship is in port. Then salute the OOD while saying 'Permission to come aboard, sir. Fireman First Class reporting for duty.' I handed over my orders and a messenger took me to meet my division officer. At last I was Ship's Company on a real ship. I met our division officer, an ensign who I did not know long as he was going off to submarine school. Another member of A Division took me down to the division compartment where I found a bunk and a locker, stowed my gear, changed into dungarees and got a very quick Cook's tour. My work station was to be in 'after diesel', which was short for After Emergency Diesel, Compressor and Pump Room. It was at the very bottom of the ship, right next to the double bottom. The actual name for the space in between was the cofferdam."

The first decommissioning of *Missouri* was set for February 1955, and just before Christmas 1954, Herb Fahr received orders transferring him from the battleship to the general communications ship, USS *Eldorado*, based in San Diego. Before leaving the *Missouri*, Fahr made a brass commemorative plaque with the names of his A Division shipmates and the date of the upcoming decommissioning on it. He riveted the plaque to the braces that supported the cables coming out of the emergency diesel generator in the A Division compartment. He took a photo of the plaque with his five-dollar Brownie, but the picture didn't come out. Some time later he learned from the *Missouri*'s captain that some workers at the Pudget Sound Naval Shipyard had stripped out all the brass they could from the ship, including Fahr's plaque.

The USS *New Jersey*, BB62.

Tirpitz

Grand Admiral Alfred von Tirpitz had won the favour of the Kaiser at an early stage in his career and with it his appointment to be Secretary of State at the German Navy Office. In 1897 he began shaping the Imperial German Navy's High Seas Battle Fleet. Tirpitz planned the fleet based on his 'risk-theory' which accepted that Britain would always be superior to Germany in fleet size, but would have to spread that larger number of vessels across the globe. The Germans, he felt, needed a battle fleet only large enough to deal effectively with that part of the British fleet that covered the English Channel and the North Sea. He estimated the size of the British Channel Fleet, and British shipbuilding capacity, and calculated that Germany would need to build sixty capital ships over the next twenty years. By June 1900, Tirpitz had secured authorization from the German Assembly to build a fleet of thirty-eight battleships, twenty large and thirty-eight smaller cruisers. By August 1914, when the First World War began, it was clear that the Tirpitz Risk Theory was incorrect. Germany's capital ship strength and capability then was less than it needed to be against that of the Royal Navy, and the gap was widening. Tirpitz soon lost the ear and the admiration of the Kaiser. He was being isolated from the naval decision-making process and in March 1916 he elected to resign.

In June 1935 an Anglo-German naval agreement was signed under which Germany agreed to restrict her fleet to 35 per cent of that of Great Britain. The Washington Treaty of 1922 and the First London Naval Conference Agreement were still in force. Under the terms of the latter agreements, capital ship displacement was limited to 35,000 tons. In 1936 Germany defied the agreed limitations, laying down her first genuine battleships since the First World War: *Bismarck*, which displaced 41,700 tons, and *Tirpitz*, displacing 42,900 tons.

From March 1942 onwards the mere presence of the battleship *Tirpitz* in Norwegian waters had caused the British to employ a large naval force to protect the Russian convoys in the North Atlantic, and to prevent the German warship from moving out into the Atlantic and becoming a greater threat. As Winston Churchill said: "She rivetted our attention." For more than two years she had not sunk a single enemy vessel or even fired on one.

When, in December 1941, Adolf Hitler became convinced that the British were on the verge of invading Norway, he demanded that Admiral Erich Raeder, Commander-in-Chief of the German Navy, redeploy his fleet there, where, according to the Führer, "the fate of the war will be decided."

Tirpitz proceeded to Trondheim on the Norwegian west coast, an ideal position from which to strike at the Russian convoys. In March of 1942, the battleship launched her first foray against a convoy, but Luftwaffe reconnaissance aircraft lost contact with the enemy convoy and *Tirpitz* was forced to withdraw to her hiding place back in the Foettenfiord, near Trondheim. On the way, she was attacked by a dozen torpedo-bearing Fairey Albacore aircraft from the Royal Navy carrier *Victorious*, but without effect. All of the torpedoes missed the battleship, which managed to shoot down two of the aircraft. In a letter to the British Chiefs of Staff, Churchill stated: "The destruction or even the crippling of this ship [*Tirpitz*] is the greatest event at sea at the present time. No other target is comparable to it. A plan should be made to attack with carrier-borne torpedo aircraft and with heavy bombers by daylight or at dawn." But *Tirpitz* was well protected by the steeply rising mountains and cliffs where she lay in the fiord, and she was defended by torpedo netting on her more exposed side. The fiord was often covered in mist and, when it wasn't, *Tirpitz* was capable of shielding herself in a smokescreen of her own making. It seemed that a level-bombing attack was the only possible method for dealing with the battleship.

In a series of futile attempts by RAF Bomber Command to destroy *Tirpitz*, the battleship was subjected to high-level attacks by Lancaster bombers using 4,000-pound blast bombs in March and April. They were augmented by Halifaxes dropping small mines in an effort to cause some of the mountainside to crumble down onto *Tirpitz*. These attacks were thwarted by the smokescreens. In three such raids, Bomber Command lost twelve heavy bombers, a rate of loss it would be unwilling to accept again for the next two years.

The very presence of *Tirpitz* in the area brought huge dividends to the Germans. In July she lay in Altenfiord on the northern tip of Norway, when the Russian convoy PQ17 passed by. British First Sea Lord Sir Dudley Pound believed [incorrectly] that *Tirpitz* was going to attack the convoy, which he ordered to scatter. In the chaos that followed, only eleven of the con-

The *Tirpitz* and her sister ship the *Bismarck* were the first genuine German battle-ships laid down since WWI.

voy's thirty-four merchant ships survived attacks by U-boats and Luftwaffe bombers.

When an attack on another convoy in January 1943 by the heavy cruiser *Admiral Hipper*, the pocket battleship *Lützow* and six destroyers, was foiled by the convoy escort, an enraged Hitler ordered that all of Germany's heavy warships be scrapped. He planned to have their big guns used on shore for coastal defence. Luftwaffe chief Hermann Goering applauded the decision, believing it to the advantage of his air force, but Admiral Raeder thought it folly and resigned over it. He was replaced by Karl Dönitz, Hitler's Admiral of Submarines. Dönitz initially supported the Führer's order, but soon changed his mind and, being more diplomatic than Raeder, was able to persuade Hitler, not only to reverse the order, but to dispatch both *Lützow* and the battlecruiser *Scharnhorst* to join *Tirpitz* in Norway. He felt that the three warships would pose a devastating new threat to the convoys. The Allies shared that view and suspended the Russian convoys through the spring and summer months, resuming them again under the protection of the increasing autumn darkness.

In September the Royal Navy launched a daring raid by six midget submarines against *Tirpitz*. Three of the subs penetrated the netting surrounding the battleship. Of these, two were destroyed, but not before laying explosives which damaged *Tirpitz* sufficiently to keep her out of action for six months, during which *Lützow* was sent to the Baltic, leaving only *Scharnhorst* in the area. The circumstances would lead to her destruction on 26 December.

Once repaired, *Tirpitz* underwent trials in Altenfiord. There she was attacked in February by Russian bombers which did no significant damage. Now the British decided to utilize their growing carrier strength in a new assault on the battleship, in which two large carriers and four escort carriers would send out 146 aircraft of various types on 3 April 1944. Barracuda dive-bombers were to spearhead the raid, with Wildcats and Hellcats in a supporting role. Top cover was to be provided by Corsairs. The first wave of the strike took off at 3 a.m. and surprised the *Tirpitz* crew, who were readying the ship for trials. With her guns largely unmanned and no time to put out a smokescreen, the battleship was extremely vulnerable. She received several hits in the attacks, and 300 of her crew were killed. But the damage was not great and *Tirpitz* was fully repaired within a month. She remained in northern Norway and continued to tie up Allied forces by her mere presence.

During August, aircraft of the Fleet Air Arm made five unsuccessful attempts to destroy the German battleship. Now the Commander-in-Chief of RAF Bomber Command, Sir Arthur Harris, was asked to do the job. He opposed any project that required him to divert bombers from his nocturnal area-bombing campaign against the cities of Germany. But he finally agreed to provide No. 617 Squadron, which had gained fame by breaching the Möhne and Eder dams in the Ruhr Valley in spring 1943. 617 was under the command of Wing Commander J.B. 'Willy' Tait. All he had to do was sink the *Tirpitz*.

Dr Barnes Wallis, the man who had designed the strange bouncing bombs used to break the Ruhr dams, was also the brains behind another innovative concept that the RAF hoped to employ against *Tirpitz*. Wallis had created what he called an 'earthquake bomb': the Tallboy, twenty-one feet long and weighing six tons, was designed to penetrate deep into the ground before exploding and creating a shock wave that would demolish all nearby structures. It was thought it should be equally effective in penetrating the deck armour of a battleship. In September1944, Bomber Command ordered two squadrons of Lancaster bombers, No. 9

and the previously selected 617, to fly their Tallboy bombloads **from** Lossiemouth in Scotland to Yagoderik near Archangel in Russia. The bomber did not have the range to carry Tallboys from their bases in Britain all the way to the Altenfiord, so the RAF elected to run the mission from a Russian base that was nearer the target. Six of the grossly overweight Lancasters were lost en route to Yagoderik.

The mission was flown on 15 September. RAF planners hoped that by having their bombers approach *Tirpitz* from an unexpected direction, the German radar operators would be confused briefly, delaying a reaction by the crew of *Tirpitz*. Such a delay, they believed, would delay the deployment of a smokescreen until it was too late to shield the battleship from the eyes of the Lancaster bomb aimers. But the *Tirpitz* crewmen did manage to lay a smokescreen before the Lancaster crews could drop their big bombs. Most of the Tallboys fell into the smoke pall, missing the battleship completely. Seven of the Lanc crews chose not to drop in the conditions, and brought their bombs back to base. The mission, however, was not a total failure. One Tallboy did hit *Tirpitz*, ruining her bow and flooding a forward section. A lengthy repair period was projected by damage assessors, so, instead of opting for the major repairs required to make her fully seaworthy again, the German Naval Staff ordered the battleship to be utilized thereafter as a floating gun battery at Tromso for the defence of northern Norway.

The Germans intended to position *Tirpitz* in shallow water at Tromso, to guard against the possibility of her being sunk or capsized in a new attack. Her Tromso berth required some dredging, however, and for the time that work took, she would be more vulnerable. Her relocation also meant that, with certain modifications, RAF bombers flying from Scotland could just reach *Tirpitz* with their Tallboys. However, the Lancs would require installation of uprated Merlin engines and the removal of some weight, including the upper gun turrets.

As the hours of daylight decreased, and with only a few days of clear weather per month, the timing of another raid on the battleship was becoming critical. Such a raid would have to be carried out no later than 26 November when daylight at Tromso would become minimal. By late October, both 617 and 9 Squadrons were again in residence at Lossiemouth, and in the early morning darkness of the 28th, thirty-two Lancasters rose sluggishly from the Scottish base, with their bomb and fuel overloads testing their performance in the extreme. Weather reconnaissance had predicted a clear spell over the target area, but the prediction was wrong. Heavy clouds obscured the battleship by the time the bombers arrived over it, and once again the attack was essentially a failure, though one bomb did some damage to the port propeller shaft of *Tirpitz* and caused some flooding of her aft compartments.

Air Vice Marshal R.A. Cochrane, in command of 5 Group, decided to attack the battleship one more time, even though such a raid would now be complicated further as the Germans had moved a group of fighters to a base near Tromso to defend *Tirpitz* against any new bombing attacks. Without their mid-upper turrets, the Lancasters would be easy prey for the German fighters during a new bombing mission. But Cochrane accepted the added risk and made a new plan for approaching the battleship undetected. He intended to bring his bombers in low, at an altitude of 1,500 feet, through a gap in the German radar network that RAF reconnaissance aircraft had located. After penetrating the German radar chain the bombers would utilize the cover of a nearby mountain range before turning north and then approaching *Tirpitz* from the east. Again, Cochrane aimed to surprise the Germans.

This time it all worked as planned. The Lancasters evaded German radar and the fighters it would have alerted, arriving undetected over the target, which was in the clear. The bombers were able to deliver their massive bombs from an altitude in excess of 10,000 feet required for the Tallboys to be effective against the heavy armour of *Tirpitz*. The ten-minute raid resulted in two Tallboy hits on the great battleship, which rolled over and capsized exposing her keel. The unorthodox ideas of Barnes Wallis had once again been proven sound, and the skill and tenacity of the air crews of 9 and 617 Squadrons had finally accomplished what had previously seemed all but impossible. More than a thousand crewmen were trapped in *Tirpitz*. Of those, fewer than 100 were rescued.

The end of *Tirpitz* marked the end of the German battle fleet. *Bismarck* and *Scharnhorst* had already been lost, and *Gneisenau* severely damaged by a mine explosion during her Channel dash from Brest early in 1942, in an RAF bombing raid on Kiel in November. *Lützow* and *Sheer* would both be sunk in April 1945, but with the loss of *Tirpitz*, the difficulty of protecting the Russian convoys was dramatically reduced for the Allies. Only two merchant ships out of 250 were lost in convoys from the fall of 1944 to the end of the war.

"Everything turns upon the Battle of the Atlantic, which is proceeding with growing intensity on both sides. Our losses in ships and tonnage are very heavy and, vast as our shipping resources which we control, the losses cannot continue indefinitely without seriously affecting our war effort and our means of subsistence."
—Winston Churchill

"We can do without butter, but, despite all of our love of peace, not without arms. One cannot shoot with butter but with guns."
—Paul Joseph Göbbels

This is war: Boys flung into a breach / Like shoveled earth; and old men,/ Broken, driving rapidly before crowds of people / In a glitter of silly decorations / Behind the boys and the old men. / Life weeps, and shreds her garments / To the blowing winds.
—Amy Lowell

The demise of *Tirpitz* following a ten-minute raid by RAF Lancasters dropping 12,000-pound Tallboy bombs on the German battleship.

Warspite

"War's spite, indeed, and we to do him right—Will call the ship he fought in 'War's-Spite."
—Queen Elizabeth I, in a 1605 play by Thomas Heywood

There have been eight ships called Warspite in the history of Britain's Royal Navy. The spelling of the name has evolved from the time of Elizabeth the First and has included Warspight, Wastspight, and Warspitt. The first *Warspite* was the vessel of the Elizabethan privateer, Sir Walter Raleigh. Armed with thirty-six guns, it was launched in 1596 at Deptford on the Thames and displaced 650 tons.

On 1 June of that year, a huge force of Royal Navy and Dutch warships set out from Plymouth to raid their Spanish enemy's port of Cadiz in an effort to destroy Spain's principal naval vessels and eliminate the growing Spanish threat to England. Raleigh, in *Warspite*, was leading one of the four Royal Navy squadrons. The British flagship was *Repulse*, under command of the Earl of Essex, who had displaced Raleigh in the Queen's affections. Raleigh hated him.

After three weeks at sea the fleet neared Cadiz. Raleigh's squadron was assigned to clear the approaches to the port of Spanish warships which might put up resistance. Meanwhile, the other squadrons of the fleet began putting hundreds of troops ashore for a direct assault on the city. On learning of this, Raleigh was enraged, knowing that in the chaos of such an attack the Spanish ships might well escape. Raleigh immediately set out to rescue the mission from the folly he saw developing.

At Elizabeth's order, command of the British fleet was shared between Essex and Lord Howard of Effingham. Raleigh rowed to the *Repulse* to confer with Essex, whom he soon persuaded to discontinue the assault on Cadiz. He then had a similar conversation with Howard who concurred. Raleigh was appointed to command an attack on Cadiz harbour in which *Warspite* would take the lead.

The next morning Raleigh's force entered the harbour and encountered a savage response from the Cadiz fortifications and the Spanish vessels. *Warspite* and many of the other British warships were badly damaged in the battle. Raleigh himself was wounded in the leg, but was utterly determined that his force would prevail and capture the Spanish treasure ships which he knew were trapped in the harbour. Essex and Howard chose instead, to plunder the town, ignoring Raleigh's insistence that their priority should be the treasure galleons. The Spaniards set fire to their treasure ships to prevent their three million pounds worth of goods being grabbed by the enemy. The British did, however, manage to capture more than twenty important Spanish vessels and 1,000 cannon before withdrawing to Plymouth. Thus went the maiden voyage of the very first *Warspite*.

The seventh *Warspite* came to be in 1912 when King George V provided names for the new *Queen Elizabeth* class of super dreadnoughts, which consisted of the lead ship and the *Barham, Valiant, Malaya* and *Warspite*. Winston Churchill, the thirty-seven-year-old First Lord of the Admiralty, was determined to establish and maintain British fleet superiority over the

Germans. In an address to the House of Commons in May, one of the first occasions in which he enlisted the language of Shakespeare and sent it to war, he sought the members' support for the new class of vessels. He described the amazing armour of the ships, up to thirteen inches thick for a new standard of protection, and the fifteen-inch main guns, together with powerful secondary six-inch guns, all vastly superior to anything the Germans had. He spoke eloquently of the oil-burning boilers that would provide the great speed, which Churchill saw as essential. It was imperative, in his view, that the new battleships be able to "curl around the head of the enemy's line and concentrate awesome firepower, shattering those vessels and throwing all the ships behind them into disarray."

Britain's naval experts confirmed that the new super dreadnoughts would have to be capable of a 25-knot speed to achieve what Churchill had described. Virtually all arguments favoured oil-fuelled power for the ships, instead of traditional coal. The speed of an oil-fired ship could be changed easily and quickly by increasing or decreasing the number of ignition sprayers activated in the boilers. An oil-powered vessel was more easily kept stable because the oil could readily be pumped from tank to tank for optimum ballasting, and an oil-powered ship could be quickly refuelled at sea, eliminating the time and inconvenience of a port call at a coaling station. In his book *The World Crisis*, Churchill stated: "As a coal ship used up her coal, increasingly large numbers of men had to be taken, if necessary from the guns, to shovel the coal from remote and inconvenient bunkers to bunkers nearer the furnaces themselves, thus weakening the fighting efficiency of the ship perhaps at the most critical moment in the battle." The advantages of oil over coal were obvious. Coaling a ship took longer and required more manpower. A full load of coal weighed more than one of oil. Oil saved weight and thus allowed for the use of bigger guns, more room for other facilities including additional boilers which meant greater speed, and other improvements including better crew facilities. Finally, the Navy's own evaluation established that the energy generated by a coal-burning battleship of *Warspite*'s displacement could not propel the vessel at anything approaching the 25-knot requirement set for her. Churchill was committed to the use of oil-fired boilers in the *Queen Elizabeth* class battleships, though many in Britain and the British government were vigorously opposed to the abandonment of coal in favour of oil. They saw the move as unpatriotic, an insult to the British coal miner, and a senseless rejection of an abundant British natural resource for one that came from a foreign, and thus vulnerable, source. The First Lord of the Admiraly sought the help of the Former First Sea Lord, Sir John Fisher, and in 1913 the Royal Commission on Oil Fuel declared in favour of oil for all new British warships and recommended the creation of fuel oil reserves sufficient for four years of fleet operation. Parliament was persuaded and the oil-burning super dreadnought programme was approved.

Churchill had to gamble on more than a switch to oil-burning for the new battleships. To achieve and maintain an advantage over the fleet of the German Kaiser, he would have to commit the new warships to being armed with new, untested fifteen-inch main guns. Again, from *The World Crisis*: "No such thing as a modern 15-inch gun existed. None had ever been made. The advance to the 13.5-inch had in itself been a great stride. Its power was greater; its life was much longer. Could the British designers repeat this triumph on a still larger scale and in a still more intense form?" The gamble might have cost Churchill his career, and left Britain largely unprepared and ill-equipped in the period leading up to war with Germany,

The keel of *Queen Elizabeth*, the lead ship of the class, was laid down at Portsmouth dockyard on 21 October 1912 and the keel-laying of *Warpite* followed ten days later at Devonport, with work beginning on *Valiant, Barham* and *Malaya* during 1913. *Warspite* was finished and fitted out early in 1915 and was put through her working-up exercises at Scapa Flow in April and May of that year. She joined the British Grand Fleet in June, engaging in North Sea sweeps preparatory to entering entering action in the war with Germany. All five *Queen Elizabeth* class vessels had completed their work-ups and were formed into the Royal Navy's new fast battleship organization, the 5th Battle Squadron, five ships which collectively mounted forty massive fifteen-inch guns.

Late in the evening of 30 May, *Warspite* sailed from Rosyth, joining the ships of the Grand Fleet to take part in the Battle of Jutland. The Executive Officer of *Warspite*, Commander Humphrey T. Walwyn, recorded events of Jutland from 2:40 p.m. of 31 May: "I realized that there was something serious doing. I passed the word round to everybody that we were in for the real thing and went round all the mess decks, and lit all action candles, etc. Saw all doors and everything closed, and went up on deck; they were just finishing washing down the weather decks. I sent all hands away to their stations and went up to the bridge to report everything ready. There was nothing in sight except our own ships, but we were steaming hard.

"Hoisted Battle Ensigns and Union Jack at after strut and masthead. Went to my action station, B turret. It was now about 4 o'clock. Got orders to load and train on Red 20. Could not see anything at all, hazy and a lot of smoke about. I made out five columns of smoke in the mist and that was all I could see—no masts or anything.

"At this point all of the principal vessels of both the German and British fleets were sailing to the southeast, and the Germans seemed to have the advantage. Their gunnery was producing results, with HMS *Indefatigable* being severely damaged, as was *Lion*, flagship of Admiral of the Fleet Sir David Beatty. Indefatigable soon exploded and sank.

"Now the ships of the 5th Battle Squadron came into play. Manoeuvring behind Beatty's ship and at a range of some 23,000 yards from their targets, *Warspite* and her sister ships quickly began to earn their keep. This part of the fight commenced when the giant guns of *Warspite* fired a few initial salvoes at one of the German light cruisers, which soon took leave.

"We were turning first to starboard, and as we came round 90 degrees I saw five enemy battle cruisers on the port bow. They were steaming the same way as we were and going very hard. I could only see their masts and the tops of their funnels above the horizon. We opened fire on number five, the *Von der Tann*, which had just destroyed the Indefatigable. I distinctly saw one salvo hit. She turned away in a cloud of black and white smoke and we turned our attention to number four, the *Moltke*."

According to German Vizeadmiral Reinhard Scheer: "Superiority in firing and tactical position were decidedly on our side until 4:19 p.m., when a new unit of four or five ships of the *Queen Elizabeth* type, with a considerable surplus of speed, drew up from a northwesterly direction and joined in the fighting. It was the English 5th Battle Squadron. This made the situation critical for our battle cruisers. The enemy fired with extraordinary rapidity and accuracy."

Just before 5 p.m., the 5th Battle Squadron came under heavy, intense fire from the German

HMS *Warspite* lies at anchor off Portsmouth.

battle cruisers. All were hit, but *Barham* and *Malaya* took the worst of it. The German vessels were also coming under extremely heavy fire and, although *Warspite* was taking several hits at the time, her executive officer remembered: "I distinctly saw two of our salvoes hit the leading German battleship. Sheets of yellow flame went right over her mastheads and she looked red fore and aft like a burning haystack. I know we hit her hard. B turret machinery working like a clockwork mouse, no hang-up of any sort whatever. *Warspite* herself was now receiving some very hard hits, with one round passing through the mess decks and the side armour. It burst in a terrific sheet of golden flame, stink and impenetrable dust. Another hit below in the side aft and began to flood the steering compartment. Yet another burst in the captain's lobby, reducing it to a state of indescribable wreckage. Farther forward, X turret was hit and water was flooding through a hole in the side and going down the engine room air supply trunk. Another took away the engineer's office."

For the next hour and a half, fire and damage control parties struggled to stabilize and repair *Warspite*, to keep her in fighting condition. During this period, *Warspite* and *Malaya* again became engaged in combat with elements of the German High Seas Fleet.

Then, as *Barham, Valiant, Warspite* and *Malaya* were manoeuvring at high speed to form up line astern of the Grand Fleet, *Warspite*'s helm suddenly jammed. Meanwhile, the British armoured cruisers *Defence, Warrior* and *Black Prince*, intent on finishing off the crippled German cruiser *Weisbaden*, had come under intense fire from the main body of the German battle fleet. *Defence* was quickly destroyed, while *Warrior* and *Black Prince* were badly damaged and vulnerable. With her rudder jammed, *Warspite* was soon turning in uncontrolled circles around *Warrior*, with the effect of shielding the cruiser from the worst of the enemy shelling, while drawing much of the fire onto herself. The sailors of *Warrior* would always be grateful to *Warspite* for the favour, whether or not it was intended, and *Warspite* would become legendary among the British people. In his book, *H.M.S. Warspite*, S. W. Roskill quotes a *Warspite* midshipman who witnessed the situation from the after torpedo control position: "Suddenly we found ourselves hauling out of the line and rushing towards the German fleet. All that we knew was that we were in a hail of fire, in fact, so much so that the salvoes falling short and over made such splashes that a lot of water came into the tower and we got quite wet. Once or twice we got a good view of the Germans, the range being only about 8,000 yards, and they looked enormous at that distance. We thought that our own six-inch guns were firing, but discovered later that it was the enemy's shells bursting on our armour belt. This had not been going on for long when the end of the world seemed to come. The deck below me seemed to open up, and I had the sensation of falling—falling."

Warspite was by now nearly unmanageable. Her captain was ordered to withdraw from the battle and take her back to Rosyth. Thus ended her involvement in the action of Jutland. Her adventure continued, however, when, as she neared port, she was attacked by U-boats and narrowly escaped two torpedoes which passed close by her bows.

Her Jutland damage repaired, *Warspite* joined with 220 Royal Navy ships, six American battleships and three French warships at the end of the First World War to take the surrender of the ten German battleships and five battle cruisers in the Firth of Forth. Following the war, only *Warspite* and her *Queen Elizabeth* class sister ships, together with the five *Royal Sovereigns*, survived a cull of the Royal Navy's main striking force. She participated in several annual cruises to the Mediterranean as part of the Atlantic Fleet and underwent her first major refit between 1924 and 1926.

With the ascent of Adolf Hitler to power in Germany during 1933, the British government authorized a major rebuilding programme for the *Queen Elizabeth* class battleships and *Warspite* remained in Portsmouth dockyard from 1934 until 1937, when she emerged thoroughly reconstructed and considerably improved.

After the start of the Second World War, in September 1939, the Royal Navy's Home Fleet came under U-boat attack in Scapa Flow when Kapitänleutnant Gunther Prien attacked and sank the great battleship *Royal Oak*. *Warspite* was immediately recalled from her Mediterranean assignment to join the Home Fleet and was sent directly to Halifax, Nova Scotia, with orders to escort slow convoy HX9, thirty ships leaving from Halifax on 18 November. In the sixth day of the crossing, she was ordered to depart the convoy and intercept the German battle cruisers *Scharnhorst and Gneisenau* in the Denmark Strait. But, in the terrible weather conditions, the German warships eluded her.

In April 1940, the German army invaded Denmark and Norway, landing troops at many Norwegian ports including Narvik in the frigid Arctic. The invasion was supported by ten Kriegsmarine destroyers. *Warspite* was again redirected, this time to meet the Home Fleet off the coast of Norway. On 10 April, British destroyers engaged and sank two of the German destroyers near Narvik. Realizing that nearly a third of the Kriegsmarine's destroyer force was trapped in port at Narvik (heavily battle-damaged and short of fuel and ammunition), the Royal Navy decided to mount an attack on the Germans, using a hunting pack of destroyers formed around *Warspite*. The raid was to be led from *Warspite* by Vice Admiral William 'Jock' Whitworth.

In a heavy swell and freezing conditions, the British force set out for Narvik at 5 a.m. on 13 April. As they approached the Norwegian port, they encountered the German destroyer *Koellner* lurking in a fiord, ready to fire its shells and torpedoes at the first British warship target to present itself. The gunners of *Warspite* sent two full broadsides from eight fifteen-inch guns and four six-inch salvoes into *Koellner*. The German vessel was literally torn apart by the barrage and sank immediately.

Earlier, a Swordfish floatplane launched from *Warspite* had been patrolling the Herjangsfiord when the pilot spotted a U-boat. It was the *U-64* and the British pilot dived to attack it with the two 250-pound armour-piercing bombs he carried. As it closed on the submarine, the Swordfish was met with 37mm anti-aircraft fire from the German boat. The biplane's observer responded with machine-gun fire and the pilot released his bombs, one of which struck and severely damaged the sub, which soon sank by the bows. She was the first German submarine to be sunk by a British naval plane in World War Two.

In Narvik harbour, the German destroyer *Giese* was trying to escape when she was shelled by some of the British destroyers. Badly damaged, she became easy prey for *Warspite*. At this point all but three of the German warships had been destroyed or run aground. The crews of the remaining three Kriegsmarine vessels ran them aground as well, abandoning them after setting scuttling charges.

After the raid, *Warspite* remained in the area as flagship for the Royal Navy task group assigned to bombard the port of Narvik preliminary to a British amphibious assault. The bombardment did not cause the Germans to surrender, as the British hoped it might, and it

HMS *Warspite* in dry-dock at Rosyth for repair of her steering control after the Battle of Jutland on 31 May 1916.

was not until 28 May that Narvik was finally captured—by elements of the French Foreign Legion. *Warspite* returned in triumph to Scapa following the Narvik battle. She would soon be off to the Mediterraneran as flagship of Admiral of the Fleet Lord Andrew Cunningham.

When Italy entered the war as Germany's ally on 10 June 1940, Admiral Cunningham in *Warspite* led his fleet in a brief sweep off Crete and the coast of Libya, looking for the Italian Navy. When France fell to the Germans on 22 June, Britain lost her naval partner in the western Mediterranean. Cunningham was now at a distinct disadvantage, seriously short of submarines, destroyers, fighter planes and minesweepers. Many of his ships were old and slow, but he had great confidence in the quality and character of his sailors, believing them to be superior to those of his Italian naval adversary. And, he had those big guns of *Warspite* and *Malaya* at his call.

In an effort to protect the vital British convoys to Malta and Alexandria, Cunningham apportioned his fleet into three groups, one being *Warspite* and five destroyers, the second consisting of the battleships *Royal Sovereign* and *Malaya* together with ten destroyers, and the third the aircraft carrier HMS *Eagle* and ten destroyers. On 7 July the three task groups departed the British base at Alexandria. They were dependent for primary reconnaissance on a picket line of British submarines in the central Mediterranean, one of which reported a very large force of Italian warships, including two battleships, steaming 200 miles east of Malta. Soon the British warships came under air attack by Italian bombers. The cruiser HMS *Gloucester* was hit and a bomb destroyed her bridge, killing her captain and twelve sailors.

In the morning of 9 July, Cunningham's fleet lay southwest of Greece. The Battle of Calabria began at 3 p.m. when the carrier HMS *Eagle* launched her aircraft in what turned out to be an ineffectual strike against some of the Italian cruisers. By 3:30 a sea battle was under way with an exchange of fire between the Italian and British cruisers. Cunningham and his fast cruisers had outrun his slower battleships, which now lagged ten miles behind him, making his position quite vulnerable. Fortunately, *Warspite* was soon able to help by sending salvoes of fifteen-inch shells into the formation of Italian cruisers, causing them to flee. The Italian battleships *Giulio Cesare* and *Conte di Cavour* began shelling *Warspite*, but their fire was inaccurate. *Warspite* returned fire with her big guns at a range of 26,000 yards and scored one critically important amidships hit on *Giulio Cesare*, which won the battle for the British. Admiral Cunningham wrote of the incident: "The *Warspite*'s shooting was consistently good. I had been watching the great splashes of our fifteen-inch salvoes straddling the target when, at 4 p.m. I saw the great orange-coloured flash of a heavy explosion at the base of the enemy's flagship funnel. It was followed by an upheaval of smoke, and I knew that she had been heavily hit at the prodigious range of thirteen miles."

The crew of the Italian battleship suffered 100 casualties and some of the vessel's boilers were destroyed, making retreat through the Straits of Messina the only course for the Italian warships. At the end of the afternoon, *Warspite* and *Eagle* came under a further Italian bombing attack near the Calabrian coast, but suffered little if any damage. After Calabria, the Italian Fleet had no interest in further contact with the Royal Navy.

By October 1940, Cunningham's warship fleet had grown in strength and capability, with *Warspite*, *Valiant*, and the new aircraft carrier *Illustrious* being supplemented by *Malaya*, *Ramillies* and *Eagle*, and joined by another *Queen Elizabeth* class battleship, HMS *Barham*.

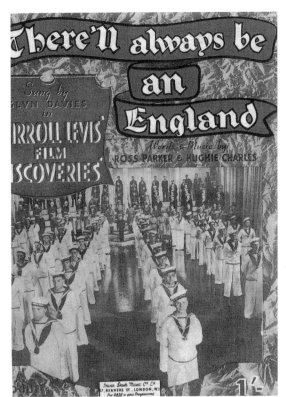

Royal Navy Admiral of the Fleet Andrew Cunningham.

Frustrated by the Italian Fleet's refusal to come out and fight, Cunningham decided to mount a raid on the key enemy ships in the harbours at the Taranto naval base. The attack was set for the evening of 11 November. *Eagle* was to participate, but mechanical problems caused her withdrawal, with some of her Swordfish aircraft being transferred to *Illustrious* for the action. Earlier that day a reconnaissance pilot overflew the Taranto harbours and confirmed the presence of all six Italian battleships, *Littorio, Cesare, Duilio, Vittorio Veneto, Conte di Cavour,* and *Doria*. The night was calm and quiet with bright moonlight as twenty-one Fairey Swordfish armed with bombs and torpedoes took off from *Illustrious*, beginning at 8:40 p.m. In an action that would cause considerably more damage to the Italian fleet than was done to the German warships at Jutland, the Fleet Air Arm planes hit *Littorio* with three torpedoes, sinking her at her moorings. They managed to sink *Conte di Cavour* and *Duilio*, each with a single torpedo hit, and heavily damaged a cruiser and two destroyers. *Warspite*, in support of the carrier operation, had played her part in one of the most dramatic actions of the war.

With the Germans poised to begin their assault on the Soviet Union, they did not need the hassle of having to rescue their Italian allies from a failed adventure in Greece and Yugoslavia, but they were compelled to do so in April 1941. To support this effort, they demanded that the Italian Navy send a battleship and supporting warships to cut supply lines between Egypt and Greece. The Germans offered air cover for the task force to protect them against more punishment from British torpedo planes.

On 27 March, Admiral Cunningham determined to take his battle fleet to sea that night from their port at Alexandria. Among his ships were *Warspite, Valiant* and *Barham*, as well as the carrier HMS *Formidable* and nine destroyers. *Warspite* was handicapped by clogged condensors and could not make more than a 20-knot top speed.

Following an initial exchange off Cape Matapan near Crete early on the 28th, between the Italians and three Royal Navy cruisers, *Gloucester, Ajax* and *Orion*, the cruisers located the battleship *Vittorio Veneto* sixteen miles north of their position. The battleship began firing her nine fifteen-inch guns at the cruisers and HMS *Valiant* quickly moved forward to take her on. *Warspite*'s condensor problem was resolved and she was soon able to join *Valiant* as they chased the fleeing *Vittorio Veneto*, which had just come under torpedo attack by Albacore bombers from *Formidable*. One torpedo struck the battleship below the waterline near one of her propellers, slowing her to a top speed of fifteen knots.

Just after 6 p.m. the *Vittorio Veneto* and her escorts were spotted forty-five miles from *Warspite*. Now the British warships were gaining on the crippled Italian battleship. Later that evening, Cunningham, who had set his mind on catching and sinking *Vittorio Veneto*, ordered eight of his destroyers ahead in pursuit of the battleship. As the night wore on, Cunningham was informed that two *Zara* class Italian heavy cruisers and a destroyer escort were nearby. The Italians were in the dark, literally, and unaware of the British fleet presence. Lacking radar, it must have been a great shock to them when they were suddenly illuminated by the searchlights of *Warspite* as she and the other British warships opened fire. Five massive shells from *Warspite*'s guns found their mark, smashing into the cruiser *Fiume* and shattering her. This was followed less than a minute later by a second salvo. At the same time, *Valiant* was busy destroying her target, the cruiser *Zara*, while *Barham* was dealing with the destroyer escort, *Alfieri*. Within the hour, three Italian warships and the cruiser *Pola*, had been sunk. The battleship *Vittorio Veneto* had escaped, but in every other sense, Matapan had been a great British victory.

After Matapan, *Warspite* experienced a series of tragic episodes which would test the mettle of her crew. With the Germans preparing a seaborne invasion of Crete, to be preceded by a paratroop assault in May 1941, warships of the Royal Navy were attempting to defend the island. On 22 May *Warspite* was sailing 100 miles west of Crete as flagship of the 1st Battle Squadron, with *Valiant*, one cruiser and ten destroyers. At 1:30 p.m. several Luftwaffe aircraft, including three Me 109s, began to attack *Warspite* from low altitude. One bomb from one of the 109s rent a 100-foot tear in the forecastle deck. A six-inch gun mount disappeared and a massive fire spread rapidly from there through a ventilation shaft to the boiler room. Thirty-eight men were killed and thirty-one wounded. Most of the battleship's starboard anti-aircraft guns had been knocked out, leaving her highly vulnerable. But the operational weapons on the port side continued blazing away at the increasing numbers of enemy dive-bombers attacking *Warspite*.

Admiral Cunningham, who had temporarily moved his headquarters ashore before this operation, signalled his ships: "Stick it out. Navy must not let Army down. No enemy forces must reach Crete by sea." The damage to *Warspite* was so severe as to be unrepairable by the drydock facilities at Alexandria, and arrangements were made for her to be repaired at the Puget Sound Naval Shipyard in Bremerton, Washington, on the west coast of the United States. In a German bombing raid on Alexandria shortly before she was due to leave for the

U.S., *Warspite* incurred additional major damage.

In the July 1943 Allied landings in Sicily, *Warspite* carried out a bombardment of enemy shore positions and, to reach her assigned station for the shelling which was to begin at 6:30 p.m., she had to hurry. A full speed of 22.5 knots was somehow achieved and, following the shelling Admiral Cunningham signalled her captain: "Operation well carried out. There is no doubt that when the old lady lifts her skirts she can run."

Off the beaches of Salerno on 15 September 1943 *Warspite* and *Valiant* were shelling German tank, artillery and troop concentrations in the nearby hills, when *Warspite* came under attack by a new and deadly weapon of the enemy, a radio-controlled aircraft glider bomb. In the early afternoon, three of the glider bombs were launched from German bombers at high altitude. One fell on *Warspite*, slamming into her amidships near the funnel. A second glider bomb then hit in the sea near her starboard side, tearing a great gap in her hull. With only partial power, she continued her shelling of the shore targets until the task was completed. Then, as she slowly steamed from the area her old chronic steering malfunction recurred and she began running in circles into a mined area. The first glider bomb had done far more damage to the battleship than most of the crew had realized. In addition to the helm trouble, she was listing five degrees to starboard, had settled four feet deeper in the water, was heavily flooded and under threat of further bombing attacks, and there was a four-foot by twenty-foot hole in her bottom. With immediate shoring and counter-flooding, the situation was somewhat eased and soon *Warspite* was taken in tow by American tugs through the Straits of Messina, shielded by a protective screen of destroyers. Through that long night the blacked-out battleship was kept afloat by the efforts of a 200-man bailing-out team. For much of the night the crippled ship swung on her tow ropes in the strong currents, completely out of control. She crept into harbour at Malta behind her tugs on 19

On the Bridge of the Flagship.

September.

Wounded and showing her age, HMS *Warspite* put to sea from Greenock on 2 June 1944 in company with the battleship *Ramillies* and several other Royal Navy warships comprising the Eastern Task Force. Their immediate destination was Plymouth, England and, from there, to just off the Isle of Wight. They were part of a force of several thousand vessels assembling in the English Channel for the Normandy invasion. *Warspite* was one of the ships assigned to provide fire support for the British troops who would be landing at Sword, one of five beaches along the French coast between Cherbourg and the Caen region. In particular, she was tasked with knocking out the German gun batteries near Le Havre. *Warspite* would have the honour of firing the opening shot of the Normandy landings at 5:30 a.m. on D-Day, 6 June. All that day the old veteran of Jutland, and so many other combat actions since 1916, continued to fire on German infantry positions and vehicle concentrations, gun emplacements and a command headquarters. Some of her gunnery was conducted with the benefit of spotting by forward observers and observation aircraft, but much of it was not. Return fire from German shore batteries frequently peppered *Warspite* with shrapnel, but she suffered no significant damage during the operation. She remained on station off shore until late in the evening when finally ordered to pull back and anchor a few miles out from Sword. On the 7th, *Warspite* resumed firing, this time at enemy strongpoints and troop concentrations.

On 8 June, her ammunition magazines nearly empty after having fired more than 300 fifteen-inch rounds, *Warspite* returned briefly to Portsmouth to reload. On the 9th she was again lying off Normandy but now in support of troops on the American invasion beaches. She took over for the battleship USS *Arkansas* which was running out of ammo. Late that day she put nearly 100 of her big shells onto an important German artillery site, winning high accolades from U.S. commanders in the area. On the 11th, she lay off Gold beach where she was asked to shell an assembly of enemy tanks and troops in a nearby wood, receiving the command "Fifty rounds, fifteen-inch, rapid fire." The action helped to save the British 50th Division from what would have been a savage counterattack.

With her main guns nearly worn out, *Warspite* was ordered back to Rosyth on 12 June to have replacement guns fitted. She sailed through the Straits of Dover and received the attentions of several German coastal gun batteries as she passed. No real harm was done, but on the 13th, off Harwich, she came too close to a magnetic mine which exploded, damaging her steering and, once again, jamming her helm. She was dead in the water and began listing to port. There were no casualties and the crew were able to correct the list through counter-flooding and restart her engines within an hour. She crawled back to Rosyth at just seven knots, arriving to the cheers of other warship crewmen.

In October 1944, *Warspite* was assigned to provide gunfire support for a British commando brigade in the final major assault of the Allied campaign in northwest Europe. The targets were German gun emplacements on the island of Walcheren near the port of Antwerp. The Allies desperately needed the port to bring in the great quantities of supplies required for their advance on Germany in the final months of the European war. It was the last time her guns were fired.

On 20 April 1947, HMS *Warspite* was off Land's End, being towed by two tugs to Gareloch in the Clyde, where she was to be cut up for scrap, when the old ship was overtaken by an incredibly violent Atlantic storm. A tow line parted and the battleship began taking on water by the bows. A new tow line was eventually attached and she was taken to Mount's Bay, Penzance, to wait out the lengthy storm. There she broke free of her anchor and soon ran aground at Prussia Cove on the far side of the bay, ripping her bows, flooding her forward compartments and sinking down by the bows. Her small caretaker crew was rescued from the threatened vessel. She lingered there, gradually disintegrating, until the summer of 1950, when she was refloated and towed to Marazion Beach near St Michael's Mount. There her remains were blasted and cut apart into sections small enough to be transported by rail to Welsh smelters. Fragments of her boilers are still buried in the beach.

The last Royal Navy warship to bear the name *Warspite* was a nuclear attack submarine of the 1960s.

We were at sea for a much longer time than it would ordinarily take to make a beeline journey from England to France. The convoy we sailed in was one of several which comprised what is known as a 'force.' As we came down, the English Channel was crammed with forces going both ways, and, as I write, it still is. Minesweepers had swept wide channels for us, all the way from England to France. These were marked with buoys. Each channel was miles wide. We surely saw there before us more ships than any human had ever seen before at one glance. And going north were other vast convoys, some composed of fast liners speeding back to England for new loads of troops and equipment. As far as you could see in every direction, the ocean was infested with ships. There must have been every type of ocean-going vessel in the world. I even thought I saw a paddle-wheel steamer in the distance, but that was probably an illusion. There were battleships and all other kinds of warships clear down to patrol boats. There were great fleets of Liberty ships. There were fleets of luxury liners turned into troop transports, and fleets of big landing craft and tank carriers and tankers. And in and out through it all were nondescript ships—converted yachts, riverboats, tugs, and barges. The best way I can describe this vast armada and the frantic urgency of the traffic is to suggest that you visualize New York harbor on its busiest day of the year and then just enlarge that scene until it takes in all the ocean the human eye can reach, clear around the horizon. And over the horizon there are dozens of times that many.
—Ernie Pyle, American war correspondent on the D-Day invasion fleet

A commemorative Royal Mail postage stamp in honour of HMS *Warspite.*

Countless are the mountains in Yamato, / but perfect is the heavenly hill of Kagu; when I climb it and survey my realm, / over the wide plain the smoke wreaths rise and rise, / over the wide lake the gulls are on the wing; / a beautiful land it is, the land of Yamato!
—from *Climbing Kaguyama and looking upon the land, Nippon Gakujutsu Shinkokai* by Emperor Jumei
The region surrounding the ancient Japanese capital of Nara was called Yamato. In time this poetic name became that of the nation.

Considered by many to have been the ultimate battleships, the World War Two giants *Yamato* and her sister ship *Musashi* were truly extraordinary. They provided the Imperial Japanese Navy with the largest guns and the heaviest armour ever employed in warships.

By the time *Yamato* was laid down in 1937, she had been the subject of twenty-three

Battleship Yamato

major proposals and revisions, each intended to refine her design to meet the exacting requirements set for her by Japanese naval planners. At 72,809 tons fully loaded, her displacement was surpassed only by that of the Cunard liner *Queen Mary*. Her four steam turbines developed 153,553 shaft horsepower and could move her through the water at up to 27.5 knots. Each of her nine eighteen-inch guns could fire two 3,240-pound shells per minute over a distance of nearly thirty miles. With a length of 863 feet and a beam of 121 feet, her basic dimensions were similar to those of the American *Iowa* class battleships *Iowa*, *New Jersey*, *Missouri*, and *Wisconsin*, though *Yamato* and *Musashi* were considerably heavier. In the 1930s Japan was set on expansion in the Pacific. To achieve it she would have to overcome the inevitable resistance of the British, with their bases and territories in the Far East, and confront the significant naval forces of the Americans already hostile towards Japan.

The battleship limitations and prohibitions of the 1922 Washington Naval Treaty spelled

the end of Japan's continuing warship programme, which called for the building of eight large battleships and eight battle cruisers. Knowing that they could not match the industrial capability of the United States, the Japanese then elected to build a small number of an entirely new class of super battleship, enormous in both size and capability. They would be vessels of such quality and superior performance that it would be virtually impossible for the Americans to reply in kind. A comparable vessel would be too large to pass through the Panama Canal, which the Japanese believed would always be a primary requirement for U.S. warships. They had estimated that the Canal could not accommodate a vessel larger than 63,000 tons with ten sixteen-inch guns and a 23-knot speed, so they instructed their planners to design a new battleship substantially larger than that. With massive armour, eighteen-inch guns and a speed of 30 knots, it would be a vessel clearly superior to anything that any potential enemy possessed or was likely to build.

The preliminary design for the new ship was ready in March 1935. With a hull 964 feet long and a displacement of 70,000 tons, she was meant to be powered by turbines generating 200,000 horsepower and a speed of 31 knots. In the next two years many tests were carried out to determine the optimum specifications and performance factors for the ship, the armour and armament. Fifty models of the new vessel were built for basin testing. After repeated revisions of the blueprints and the reduction of the speed requirement to 27 knots in 1937, the final design was completed and construction began.

Work on the new class of Japanese battleships was to be done in utmost secrecy at the Nagasaki, Kure, Yokosuka and Sasebo shipyards. As it happened, the slipways of the Nagasaki yards were clearly visible from both the American and British consulates there. Thus, the first task for the builders was the erection of a large warehouse to obscure the view from the consulates, followed by the erection of 75,000 square metres of hemp screening which completely surrounded the slipways. Engineering and construction then proceeded under the tightest security. The few lapses and infringements were dealt with harshly and, while the West was aware that something special was going on in the shipyards, little if any significant intelligence was gathered about the specifics of the project.

Size mattered in several important ways with the new battleships. Their immense hulls, for example, could not be manoeuvred in the water by the use of conventional tugs, so a new, purpose-built 1,600 hp tug had to be designed and constructed. To deliver the extremely heavy armament from the Kure Naval Arsenal to the Nagasaki yards, a specially constructed freighter was needed. *Yamato* was assembled in a drydock at the Kure Kaigun Kosho yards, but the hull of her sister ship, *Musashi*, would have to be launched down a slipway. Japanese engineers knew from their analysis of launch data from the *Queen Mary* and other large-hull vessels that *Musashi* might gain too much momentum as she left the slipway and continue across the harbour to run aground on the opposite shore. On the day of the launch, however, they were able to control the momentum through the use of special friction chains, though the hull still caused a wave so large that it flooded some houses on the bank.

The Type 94 eighteen-inch guns of the *Yamato* class battleships were ranged by a complex of three 49-foot rangefinders mounted high on the tower superstructure with the fire director. Each of the three triple turrets weighed 2,774 tons, roughly equivalent to the weight of a large destroyer. The ship carried a total of 900 projectiles for the great guns, or 100 for each gun. At an elevation of forty degrees a shell took 89 seconds to reach its target at a distance of 40,000 yards. The blast effects when the main armament was fired were catastrophic to anyone caught topside in an exposed position. In a test experiment, guinea pigs in cages were positioned on deck when the main guns were fired and the poor animals were disintegrated by the shock wave. The *Yamato* vessels were also mounted with a mix of fifty-two anti-aircraft and anti-torpedo boat guns and the latest radar, sonar arrays and electronic equipment. Each battleship carried seven Aichi E13A 'Jake' or Mitsubishi F1M2 'Pete' float-planes. These aircraft were launched from two 63-foot catapults. They were retrieved from the water by a six-ton 60-foot crane and were stowed in a hangar near the stern. The aircraft were used for general purpose and long-range reconnaissance. *Yamato* was the heaviest armoured vessel ever built. The weight of her armour plating alone was 22,895 tons; twenty-two-inch armour protected her barbettes. All of her vital areas were covered by sixteen-inch armour, each sheet of which weighed sixty-eight tons. It was sloped outwards to help deflect falling shells and was intended to defeat eighteen-inch enemy shells, though no such threat existed from any other naval power, when fired from a range beyond 22,000 yards The hull armour extended down to the bottom plates with a slight bulge to cope with the

Yamato is targetted by U.S. Navy conventional and torpedo bombers on 7 April 1945. She sank at 2:23 p.m. with the loss of 2,598 of her crew.

The listing and heavily damaged Japanese battleship *Ise* in August 1945. After the loss of four aircraft carriers off Midway Island in June 1942, the Japanese began the conversion of *Ise* and her sister ship *Hyuga* to hybrid battleship-carriers. Both warships took part in the Battle of Leyte Gulf. They ended the war out of fuel and stranded near Kure where they were attacked by Allied planes and sunk in the shallows.

force of torpedo explosions. With her 7.8-inch armoured deck, she was theoretically protected against even a 2,200-pound armour-piercing bomb dropped from 10,000 feet. Her great hull contained a network of more than 1,150 flood-control watertight compartments.

The designers of *Yamato* utilized fifty experimental hull models in their tests at the Tokyo Naval Technical Research Centre, which contained the largest marine test basin in the country. The purpose of the testing was to find ways to increase hull efficiency and minimize resistance in order to achieve the desired speed and performance for the massive new warship. One conclusion resulting from the experiments was that a huge and bulbous bow forefoot would have to be adopted to aid in reducing hull resistance and achieving the required 27-knot speed capability. In actual trials, *Yamato* reached a speed of 27.46 knots. Another important characteristic of her hull design was a rather shallow draught which would allow her to utilize most of the existing drydock and base facilities of the Imperial Japanese Navy.

Having been laid down on 4 November 1937, the battleship *Yamato* was launched on 8 August 1940. Her main engines had been fitted in September-November 1939, with her boilers going in between May and October of that year. Between May and July of 1941, the main gun armament was fitted and on 16 December 1941, she was commissioned and became part of the 1st Battleship Division of the Imperial Japanese Navy and training in her commenced. The next significant event in her career came on 12 February 1942 when she became the flagship of Admiral Isoroku Yamamoto, Commander-in-Chief, Combined Fleet IJN. The Battle of Midway, 3-6 June 1942, was her first major combat engagement and, as Yamamoto's flagship, she became the Japanese command centre for the battle. Midway Island was an American naval air base and refuelling station located 1,136 miles west of Hawaii.

Yamamoto wanted to draw out and destroy the U.S. Navy aircraft carriers from Pearl Harbor and the confrontation would take place in the area of Midway. Japanese naval forces outnumbered the U.S. forces substantially, with eight aircraft carriers, eleven battleships, eighteen cruisers and fifteen destroyers, against America's three aircraft carriers, no battleships, eight cruisers, and fifteen destroyers. In the event these superior numbers did not help the Japanese. Midway was an air battle between Japanese and U.S. carrier-based aircraft and a major defeat for the IJN. They suffered the loss of four aircraft carriers *Kaga, Akagi, Hiryu* and *Soryu*, in their first naval defeat since 1592. The U.S. Navy lost the carrier *Yorktown*. From the Battle of Midway on, Japanese aircraft carriers were no longer a significant threat to American forces and after the battle the capability of both Japanese and U.S. fleets was roughly comparable, enabling the U.S. to begin an offensive role in the Pacific war. In this major air fight, the big guns of *Yamato* did not come into play and after the battle, she returned to Japan's Inland Sea. By this point the Japanese admirals had begun to accept the spreading belief that the aircraft carrier had supplanted the battleship as the key naval weapon. They ordered the immediate conversion of *Shinano*, the third *Yamato* class battleship, then under construction, to a heavy aircraft carrier.

In August 1942, *Yamato* was sent to Truk in the Solomon Islands to participate, with *Musashi* in a campaign to recapture Guadalcanal from the Americans. The recently completed *Musashi* arrived in the area on 22 January 1943 and became the new flagship of Admiral Yamamoto on 11 February. Now the Japanese were rapidly losing ground in the Solomons and were forced to abandon Guadalcanal. On 18 April, over the island of Bougainville, P-38 fighters of the 5th U.S. Army Air Force intercepted and shot down a Japanese bomber carrying Admiral Yamamoto. The admiral died in the crash and his ashes were returned to Tokyo aboard *Musashi*. After a refit, both *Yamato* and *Musashi* returned to Truk where, on 25 December, *Yamato* was struck by a torpedo fired from the U.S. submarine *Skate*, causing flooding in her upper powder magazine near the number three main turret and necessitating another return to Japan for repairs.

By mid-May 1944, the main Japanese fleet had become an aircraft carrier strike force with a supporting battleship group which included *Musashi* and *Yamato*. On 9 July the battleships went to Lingga anchorage to train in preparation for the coming defence of the Philippines. On 22 October both *Yamato* and *Musashi* moved swiftly through the Philippines to launch an attack on the U.S. fleet in Leyte Gulf. The next day the Japanese heavy cruisers *Atago* and *Maya* were the victims of American submarines off Palawan Island and Admiral Kurita transferred his flag from *Atago* to *Yamato*.

The two giant battleships came under heavy air attack on 24 October, with *Musashi* receiving twenty torpedoes and many bombs in the four-hour raid. *Yamato* took just three bomb hits, none of which caused serious damage, but her sister ship had been mortally wounded and went down with the loss of 1,039 crewmen. On the following day *Yamato* engaged in what would be her only battle with enemy vessels, firing 104 salvoes of her massive shells and sinking one American escort carrier, the USS *Gambier Bay*, and a destroyer in the Battle of Samar Gulf. The IJN lost the battle and with it the Philippines. *Yamato* left the area for Brunei Bay in Borneo and from there returned to Japan.

The last important stop in the Allied island-hopping campaign of the war was Okinawa, an island group of the central Ryukus, in the East China Sea about fifty miles southwest of the southernmost Japanese island, Kyushu. Okinawa was serving as a base for the last-ditch Kamikaze attacks which were attempting to halt the Allied drive on Japan. U.S. naval forces assaulted the main island in Operation Iceberg, the most complex Allied invasion landing of the Pacific war, on Easter Sunday, 1945. Fleet Admiral Chester W. Nimitz was in overall command of 1,500 ships and 250,000 men.

Yamato was now called on to perform one of two final assisgnments. She was ordered to Okinawa to destroy the enemy invasion fleet with her big guns or, failing that, she was to be run aground there and use her great firepower in support of the Japanese defenders. The plan had originated with Admiral Soemu Toyada, the new Commander-in-Chief of the Combined Fleet. While the Japanese believed *Yamato* to be virtually unsinkable, the assignment was, on any realistic assessment, suicidal. She was to attempt it against the opposition of many Allied aircraft and warships with little or no Japanese air cover.

Yamato sailed at 3 p.m. on 6 April 1945 from Tokuyama Bay on Japan' Inland Sea. She was part of a task force commanded by Vice-Admiral Seiichi Ito, and was only fuelled for a one-way trip to Okinawa, but carried a full load of ordnance for her armament. At 10 a.m. the next day, her radar showed enemy aircraft in the area and her crew was put on a high state of readiness for attack. Just after noon, two large groups of American carrier aircraft were sighted approaching the task force and the battleship was ordered to a speed of 24 knots. Shortly before 12:30 p.m., she was struck by three torpedoes on the port side and by three bombs near the number three turret. Substantial damage was done to the flying deck and to many of the smaller guns. Additional bombs hit her in the next five minutes and a large fire was started.

There was a lull in the attacks lasting about forty minutes. At approximately 1 p.m. *Yamato* was struck by three more torpedoes on the port side and by one on the starboard side. She began a severe list to port, which was largely corrected by counter-flooding of many compartments. Two of her boiler rooms, one engine room and one hydraulic machinery room were flooded and her speed now fell to 18 knots.

Ensign Mitsuru Yoshida was Assistant Radar Officer serving in *Yamato*. In his book, *Requiem For Battleship Yamato*, translated by Richard H. Minear, Yoshida recalled life aboard the great ship, and her last days: "I was an average OCS officer, a run-of-the-mill military man. Among the countless young men sent into battle at the end of the Pacific war, I was entirely unremarkable. It is only that the experience I was confronted with was unique, nothing more.

"29 March, early morning: over the ship's P.A.—'Preparations for getting under way commence at 0815 hours; getting under way is scheduled for 1500 hours.' There has never been so sudden a sailing. Is this it? From the communications people, reports that wireless and signal traffic is heavy. This is it—the sortie we've been waiting for. Being anchored 'in preparation for entering the dock' was in fact a cover for our imminent departure.

"When I first came on board, a novice, an officer drafted out of college, I found a four-hour watch very demanding. Without a moment's let-up, one must maintain close watch over everything around the ship and keep an eye on the movement of other ships at anchor; in addition, one must plan, implement, and inspect the daily schedule on board. The junior officer of the deck must always function on the double; walking will not do.

"About 0100 hours: A single B-29 passes directly over *Yamato*. 'Continue refueling, but man anti-aircraft batteries.' The plane is much too high, so we do not fire. The tenacity with which this ship is being reconnoitered is enough to make us gnash our teeth. Day after day the American reconnaissance planes have come in a diligent effort to capture *Yamato*'s movements. And they have not missed the golden opportunity offered by this refueling for the mission.

Once more we check that hatches, doors, and covers have been sealed. The work of getting ready is almost completed. In the midst of growing tension on board, all remains calm. Time hangs heavy.

"The ship's P.A.: "The deadline for mail is 1000 hours.' Even though we are in no mood for it, we all encourage each other and try to write home. How difficult to write a letter to be read after one's death! But I must requite those kind enough to hope for even a single word written by me. What to do about mother's grief? Is there any way that I, unfilial in dying ahead of her, can now console her?

"My place of duty is in the middle of the bridge, the heart and brains of the ship; my duty is to supervise the lookouts stationed at sixteen places on board and to evaluate their reports, deciding which to pass on to the staff officers, from the captain on down. When we are steaming on alert, it is a most important duty.

"*Yamato* advances inexorably, throwing up a bow wave to either side. Thanks to the incomparable seaworthiness of the ship's construction, there is no pitch or roll; even on the bridge, we have the illusion of standing on firm ground.

"The broad outlines of the operation are as follows. First, all ships will charge ahead, attract

The bridge and superstructure of the Japanese battleship *Nagato* which is being inspected by U.S. Navy personnel in August 1945. The big warship did not fire her main guns in combat until the Battle of Leyte Gulf in October 1944, where she suffered light damage. After the war, in mid-1946, *Nagato* was a target in the nuclear weapons testing, Operation Crossroads and was sunk in the second round of the tests.

the American naval and air forces, and open the way for the success of the special attack planes. Any ship still afloat will simply press forward into the very midst of the enemy until she runs aground; all hands will fight with might and main until all ammunition is expended. Then any men still alive with one bound will become foot soldiers and join the fray. Hence machine-guns and pistols have been distributed to each division.

"Breakfast. Probably the last meal we can enjoy in a normal atmosphere. I cannot bear to eat it inside this gloomy compartment. I scramble up the ladder outside the radar compartment, come out atop the platform of the antenna used in sending out transmissions, a flat area a little more than two metres square. I take a big bite out of my ball of rice. An ideal spot, surrounded by sky. When the sea wind blows up and threatens to knock me off, I hold on by wrapping my legs around the support.

"1200 hours. We have just reached the halfway point. The entire task force advances serenely. The commander in chief looks to each side of him and smiles a broad smile: 'We got through the morning all right, didn't we?'

"These are his first words since the mission began, when he took his seat in front and to the right of the bridge. The sequence of alerts, the choice of zig-zag, the speed, the changes of course—he has left everything to the captain of *Yamato*; and he has merely nodded silently in response to the reports of his chief of staff.

"From now on, until the ship capsizes, he will sit, arms folded, like a rock amid the smoke of the guns and the rain of bullets. All those around him will be killed or wounded, but he will move not at all.

"Was he too proud to assert control over this operation, forced through over his opposition, opposition so strong he risked losing his command? Or was this his silent protest against the fate of being remembered as the highest-ranking officer of an operation that will live in naval annals for its recklessness and stupidity? A man of refreshing directness, the tall and graceful Admiral Ito."

At 1:45 p.m. yet another series of attacks began and this time the giant battleship took at least two torpedoes to port and one to starboard. Now she was listing up to eighteen degrees to port and the list was increasing rapidly. Additional counter-flooding was ordered but the degree of list continued to grow. The ship was moving through the water at barely ten knots, steaming in a giant circle. By 2 p.m. all power failed in *Yamato* and the captain ordered that the crew make ready to abandon ship. The great vessel began to capsize and shortly thereafter, an immense explosion of the stern ammunition magazines was followed immediately by a secondary blast which ripped the ship apart. The huge smoke cloud was visible 110 miles away on Kagoshima Island.

In the campaign for Okinawa, which was finally secured by U.S. forces on 22 June, more than 12,000 Americans were killed. Japanese dead amounted to just over 110,000, including 24,000 civilians. The Japanese lost sixteen ships sunk, with four damaged, while the Americans lost thirty-six ships, with 368 damaged. The Americans lost several hundred aircraft and the Japanese several thousand.

The end came for *Yamato* at 2:23 p.m., 7 April, when she sank taking 2,498 of her crew with her. Only 280 survived. The Japanese Navy of the Second World War was no more. It marked the end of the ultimate battleship and nothing like her was ever attempted again.

After World War Two

By 1946, when HMS *Vanguard* was commissioned, the battleship era had nearly finished. The Second World War had clearly demonstrated that the aircraft carrier would now be the new capital ship of the world's navies.

Seven years earlier, however, there had been much talk in Royal Navy circles of building a new, "one-off" battleship which would utilize the fifteen-inch guns that had been removed from the old light battle cruisers *Glorious* and *Courageous* in the 1920s, when they were converted into aircraft carriers. These guns and their turrets had been held in reserve for the *Queen Elizabeth* and *Revenge* class battleships. In March 1939, Sir Stanley Goodall, Director of Naval Construction, wrote a proposal suggesting that the guns be the basis for a new battleship. He argued that the precious time spent in designing, constructing and testing main-battery guns and turrets for the new vessel could be saved. All the significant European navies appeared to be using fifteen-inch guns in their newest battleships. Actually, the fifteen-inch main guns mounted in Germany's *Bismarck*, Italy's *Vittorio Veneto*, and France's *Richelieu* were all capable of shooting to a substantially greater range than those intended for the new British battleship.

Goodall believed that the new warship should be based on a hull utilizing the armour standards of the *King George V* class, with a *Lion* class propulsion system. As well as the eight fifteen-inch guns, in four turrets, the new battleship, *Vanguard*, would carry sixteen 5.25-inch guns in eight mounts, forty-eight two-pounder pom-poms and two spotting aircraft. She was to be capable of between 27 and 31.5 knots. Her vertical armour protection was intended to resist fifteen-inch 1,938-pound shells fired at a range of 14,000 yards. Horizontal protection was meant to resist 1,000-pound armour-piercing projectiles dropping from 14,000 feet. Her hull would be designed to resist the explosion of a 1,000-pound charge of TNT. Her fully-loaded displacement would be 51,400 tons.

It was believed that *Vanguard* would be needed to help counter the growing Japanese naval capability in the Far East, where, it had been estimated, Japan would be operating at least four more capital ships than the Royal Navy by 1944. *Vanguard* would be assigned to help protect British trade routes in Australasian and Indian waters, and to serve as a stop-gap show of force until a Royal Navy battle fleet could arrive.

In May 1940 the design of *Vanguard* was approved and her keel was laid at the John Brown & Company yard on the Clyde on 2 October 1941. However, with highest construction priority going to Britain's newest aircraft carriers, the *Illustrious, Implacable, Majestic* and *Colossus* class vessels, it was not until early 1944 that *Vanguard* gained a top priority status. She was launched on 30 November 1944 and was sponsored by HRH Princess Elizabeth, the eighteen-year-old future Queen, in one of her first important public appearances. "I am very proud to come here to launch this truly magnificent addition to the Royal Navy. You may be sure I shall always follow the movements of this fine ship and of all who serve in her with the greatest possible interest. When I first saw her I found it hard to realise that this vast structure, now safely afloat, is the work of men's hands. The men and women of this shipyard may indeed feel proud of this evidence of their patience, their skill, and their hard work through many months. They must surely have put something into her which is part of the

U.S. Navy F4U Corsair fighters
returning from a combat mission
during the Korean War in
September 1951. They are passing
the carrier USS *Boxer*.

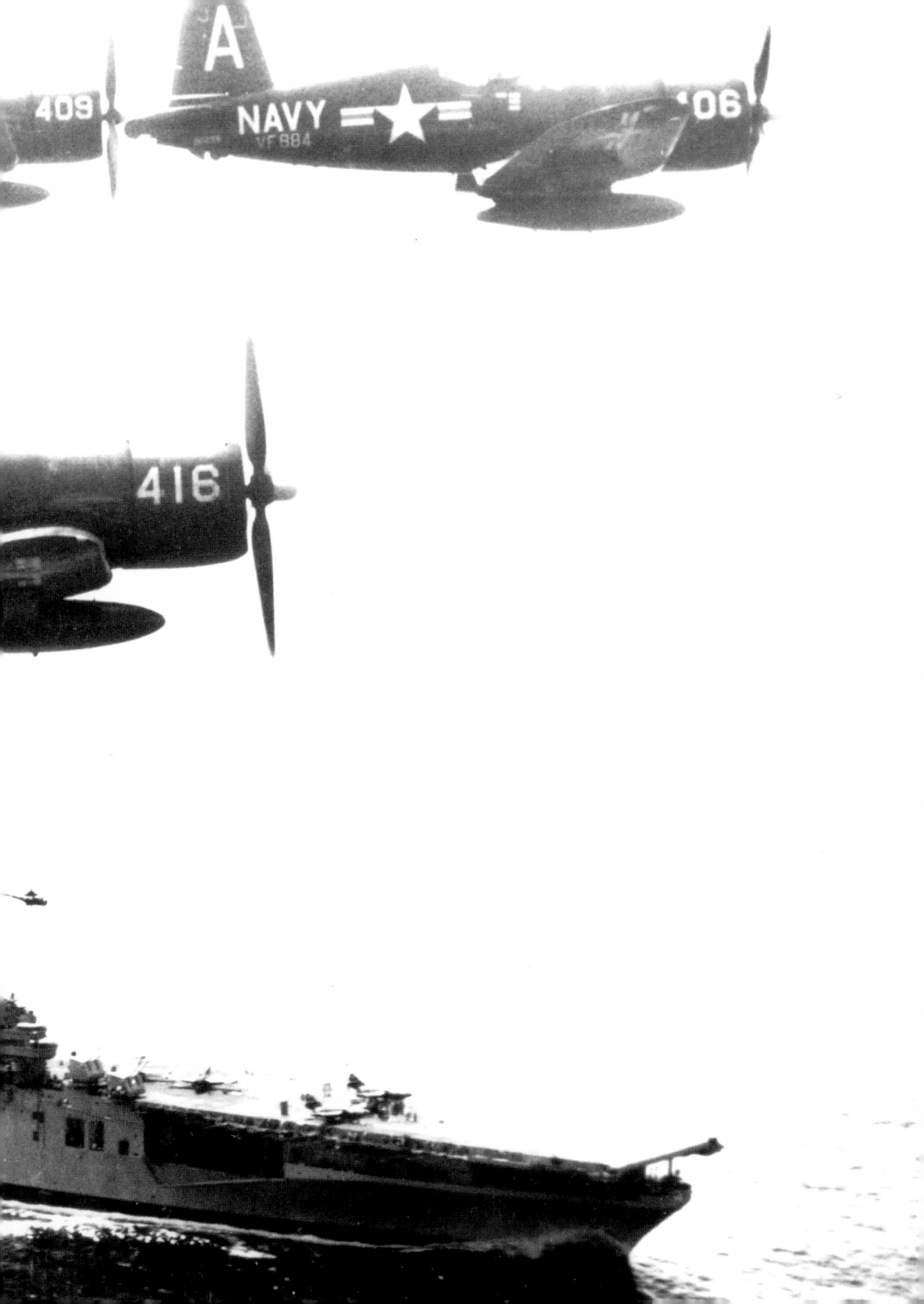
A
409
NAVY
VF884
06
416

staunchness of our race."

Deriving from the French "avant-garde", the word vanguard refers to "the foremost position in an army or a fleet advancing into battle", and the motto of HMS *Vanguard* was "We Lead". Similar in appearance to the battleships of the earlier *King George V* class, *Vanguard* was fully fitted out and left the John Brown yard on 2 May 1946, the ninth Royal Navy warship to be called *Vanguard*. The tenth *Vanguard* was to be a nuclear-powered ballistic missile submarine which was laid down in September 1986 and launched in March 1992. The 15,000-ton sub was armed with sixteen Trident D5 intercontinental ballistic missiles and was also fitted with four torpedo tubes. Together with her sister ships, *Vigilant*, *Vengeance* and *Victorious*, this last *Vanguard* leads Britain's nuclear deterrent capability.

Vanguard was the last battleship of the Royal Navy. She did not, in the end, utilize the eight fifteen-inch guns originally fitted to HMS *Glorious* and HMS *Courageous*. What she did incorporate were the four main turrets from these old ships, giving her thick turret armour. In these turrets were mounted fifteen-inch Mk I guns which fired a 1,938-pound shell with a 2,458fps muzzle velocity, but her crews never fired her guns in anger.

To some extent, the design of *Vanguard* was influenced by lessons learned with the loss of the Royal Navy battleship *Prince of Wales*, which sank on 10 December 1941 in the South China Sea following an attack by Japanese land-based aircraft. Specifically, major improvements were made in such areas as pumping facilities, internal watertight subdivisions, additional diesel generators and escape routes from the lower compartments.

Finally completed and commissioned in late 1946, *Vanguard* was the last British dreadnought battleship and the only one never to go to war. In a three-month tour of South Africa by *King George VI*, she operated as the royal yacht and in 1949 was assigned to the Mediterranean Fleet. She served as a training vessel from summer a proposal was floated to convert *Vanguard* into a guided missile warship, but the plan was shelved as unaffordable. The battleship entered the Reserve Fleet in 1956 and, in August 1960, she was sent to Shipbuilding Industries, Faslane, for scrapping.

On 12 May 1951, the newly recommissioned USS *New Jersey* (BB62) arrived in Yokosuka, Japan, recalled to active duty for the Korean War. North Korean communist troops had invaded South Korea in June 1950 and *New Jersey* was being reactivated to join her sister ship *Missouri* in bombarding the North Korean enemy. When the North Koreans had moved south, *Missouri* had been pulled from her midshipman training assignment and dispatched to Korea. Within two months, she was re-equipped and on station there.

The United Nations had agreed to oppose the North Korean invasion of its southern neighbour, but was unsure of North Korea's military capability. The only certainty was that there would be jet fighters on both sides capable of flying at much higher speeds than their World War Two fighter counterparts. A major concern of the U.S. Navy was that the Soviet Union and China would provide enough front line aircraft to the North Koreans to create an air defence nightmare for the Navy. As it happened, that concern was not justified. At the time, however, it was believed that the American carriers would require protective cover from the remaining *Iowa* class battleships.

Missouri and *New Jersey* went to war in Korea looking essentially the same as they had in World War Two. The only major equipment changes were the addition of new, advanced radar and electronics for greater efficiency in detecting and identifying air and surface targets, as well as assisting in the direction of air strikes. The single major change to the armament of the reactivated *Iowa* class ships was the programme to add automatic three-inch/.50 calibre medium range anti-aircraft guns, to replace many of the quadruple 40mm mounts.

The first job given *New Jersey* was to provide anti-aircraft cover for the *Essex* class carriers of Task Force 77 off the Korean coast. While on this mission, the battleship was detached from the task force to bombard North Korean shore installations and enemy supply movements. She gradually proceeded northward to Wonsan harbour, where her main guns were fired at the enemy transportation centre there through the night of 20-21 May. The next morning began with North Korean artillery shelling the battleship. Some relatively minor damage was caused when an enemy round hit turret one, destroying a periscope there. The ship's crew was ordered to battle stations. The shelling continued and, on the battleship's port side, Seaman Robert Osterwind was mortally wounded when shrapnel fragments from an exploding round struck him in the chest. Osterwing became the only man ever to be killed in action on the *New Jersey*.

When the Army of the Republic of Vietnam (ARVN) was unable to cope with the North Vietnamese communist insurgents in 1965, the United States sent a large ground force into South Vietnam in an attempt to stabilize the situation. Once again, the U.S. Navy was called on to provide fire support and air cover in that region. Internal squabbling in the Navy between proponents of battleship reactivation and the naval aviation community, including the Chief of Naval Operations at the time, caused a nearly two-year delay in the next recommissioning of the USS *New Jersey*. Then, on 31 July 1967, the CNO retired and the very next day the Navy announced that *New Jersey* would be reactivated for deployment in Vietnam. *New Jersey* got the nod over her *Iowa* sisters because she was the nearest to combat-ready of the four vessels.

Despite the decision to bring *New Jersey* back for service in Southeast Asia, there remained a feud within the Navy. The air community felt threatened by the presence of the battleship and resented the funding it was drawing. The Marine Corps, though, mindful of the support it needed from the old warship, lent its considerable support to the involvement of *New Jersey* in the Vietnam conflict. The Department of Defense, moreover, took the view that the battleship offered the capability of hitting many of the targets normally assigned to aircraft, without suffering the losses normally incurred in pilots and aircraft on those assignments.

New Jersey is credited with having achieved an outstanding level of performance in Vietnam. Operating all along the coast there, with virtual impunity, the battleship was considered extremely effective in the destruction of important targets within range of her big guns. Her intimidating presence caused the Vietcong force to move well inland, easing pressure on South Vietnamese troops near the coast. Yet, by 1969, this same power to intimidate by her very presence was seen as a problem by the new Nixon administration in Washington. Though she was scheduled for a second deployment to Vietnam in September, the White House ordered that she be deactivated instead, along with 100 other Navy ships. Washington, it seems, was concerned that the threatening shape of *New Jersey* off the Vietnamese coast

below: HMS *Vanguard* in Gibraltar's
Number One drydock for an overhaul.

would impede peace negotiations and prolong the war. As it happened, both the peace talks and the war went on and on, and in 1972 the North Vietnamese launched a major spring offensive and stalled the peace negotiations, causing the U.S. president to resume significant offensive operations against the North. It seems probable that, had the battleship not been mothballed at the end of her first deployment to Vietnam, she could have contributed importantly to the action against Haiphong harbour and other vital targets in the North.

All four *Iowa* class battleships participated in action during World War Two and the Korean War, but *New Jersey* was the only battleship to participate in the Vietnam War. She also saw action when ordered to the Mediterranean to fire on Syrian anti-aircraft batteries in Lebanon from December 1983 through February 1984. Now she had been re-equipped to carry thirty-two Tomahawk cruise missiles, sixteen Harpoon anti-surface missiles, four Vulcan-Phalanx close-in "Gatling guns" for air defence; a cruiser-style communications system; aviation facilities and operating stations for SH-60B helicopters; updated air and surface radars; and conversion of the fuel plant to burn Navy distillate fuel.

In December 1989 a battle group led by the USS *New Jersey* steamed into the Persian Gulf region, the single aircraft carrier battle group headed by the USS *Midway* that had been stationed there. *Midway* had been patrolling the Indian Ocean just outside the Persian Gulf, guarding the strategic oil waterway where more than 500 commercial vessels had been destroyed or damaged during the eight-year Iran-Iraq war. For the first time since 1986, the region was without the air-strike capability of a U.S. carrier. Iran called the arrival of the *New Jersey* provocative and an act of aggression. Saudi Arabia showed her displeasure at the presence of the battleship by refusing to allow a port call. Instead, *New Jersey* was given a warm, if low-key, welcome by the island state of Bahrain where she anchored two miles off the coast and much of the 1,800-man crew went ashore for a brief liberty visit. Most of the Gulf Arab states were balancing a quiet support for an American military presence with their overt neutrality and opposition to such a foreign presence in the region.

New Jersey was the largest warship ever to enter the Gulf and sail the Strait of Hormuz.

The crew of the USS *Missouri* (BB63) reacted with stunned silence as their captain informed them unofficially on the internal television system that their ship was soon to be decommissioned and retired. It was 1990, and before decommissioning could take place, it was cancelled as the United States suddenly began preparations for war. In November, the *Missouri* was ordered to join her sister ship, the USS *Wisconsin* (BB64), in the Persian Gulf. Having had major refits, the two *Iowa* class battleships were armed with Tomahawk cruise missiles capable of striking strategic inland targets, in addition to their massive sixteen-inch main guns for shore bombardment.

In the mid-morning of 16 January 1991, Captain Albert Lee Kaiss, who would be the last captain of the *Missouri*, and the last battleship captain in the world, received orders to prepare a cruise missile strike. Fourteen hours later, just after midnight, Kaiss ordered reveille to be sounded and told his crew to go to the head because everyone would be ordered to general quarters in about ten minutes and "we are going to general quarters for real. We are currently in receipt of a strike order, and we are making preparations to launch Tomahawks in the next hour."

On 2 August, Iraqi President Saddam Hussein had sent three Iraqi army divisions into neighbouring Kuwait, taking over the tiny nation and threatening Saudi Arabia to the south. With U.S. Navy warships under way to the Gulf, President George Bush ordered Operation Desert Shield, a mobilization for action in that region. An Allied coalition began forming, and American congressional debates were held; economic sanctions and United Nations resolutions were sought in preparation for conflict with Iraq.

By October *Missouri* was in San Diego where some of her crew underwent specialist training at Navy schools. Training continued aboard the battleship as she headed to the Persian Gulf. On the morning of 16 January 1991, *Missouri* was at anchor in Bahrain when Desert Shield became Desert Storm, the Gulf War proper.

At 1:40 a.m. the first Tomahawk missile blasted from an armoured box launcher in *Missouri*'s superstructure, creating a bright white halo and a tail of orange flame as it skidded and lifted into the blackness. The battleship fired six Tomahawks into Iraq that night. By 20 January, the *Missouri* Tomahawk team had launched a total of twenty-eight of the precision guided missiles at Iraqi targets.

Off Khafji on 3 February, *Missouri* was called on to fire her sixteen-inch main guns in anger for the first time since March 1953 off Korea. Her task was to target concrete command and control bunkers and the terrain required the battleship to manoeuvre much closer into shoal water than safety considerations normally allowed, where there was as little as three feet of water under her keel.

This bunker targetting assignment involved the first combat use of the remotely piloted reconnaissance and scouting vehicle (RPV) system from *Missouri*. The small, pilotless aircraft was "flown" by a controller on the 0-3 level of the battleship via a television monitor and a remote control box similar to that used by flyers of powered model aeroplanes. The little RPV was fitted with a black-and-white television camera and an infra-red sensing system for sending a high-resolution video image at night. It was recovered aboard the ship with the aid of a net strung between poles on the fantail.

For three nights the main guns of the *Missouri* fired into the Khafji area, delivering a total of 112 of the huge rounds. The ship was relieved by *Wisconsin*, for one week, and then returned to Khafji to shoot an additional sixty rounds of the big stuff in nine fire-support assignments. The targets included infantry battalions, a command bunker, a mechanized unit and an artillery battery, all with the considerable assistance of the RPV whose television pictures were shown on hundreds of monitors throughout the battleship.

In those and subsequent bombardment assignments, *Missouri*'s World War Two-era plotting room computers worked well, helping her gun crews to achieve great accuracy.

The ground war began on 24 February. *Missouri* was tasked with firing into Iraqi-held territory in support of the operation to re-take Kuwait. She was part of an effort to fool the Iraqis into believing that a coalition amphibious landing in Kuwait was imminent. She pretended to be two battleships, frequently moving along the shore and laying down a massive bombardment to make the enemy think that they were exposed to twice the firepower. She fired 133 rounds in two hours on the night of 25 February. During the firing, the officer of the deck spotted an orange fireball that was glowing as it grew larger and nearer to the ship. Captain Kaiss recognized it as an incoming missile and the OOD ordered everyone to hit the deck. For nearly two minutes from the officer's warning, the entire crew of *Missouri* waited for the impact and many of them watched as other ships in the area fired several chaff rockets intended to decoy the radar seeker of the enemy missile. It was a Chinese-built Iraqi Silkworm anti-ship missile and it approached the stern of the battleship, crossing from starboard to port and then seeming to head down the port side. At that instant, two white streaks, Sea Dart missiles fired from the British destroyer HMS *Gloucester* at a range of four miles intercepted the Silkworm; one of them detonated it, probably saving *Missouri* from damage and possibly worse. After the Silkworm attack, an RPV was launched from *Missouri* to locate the site of the enemy missile battery. That accomplished, the battleship began firing its heavy projectiles at the enemy site, quickly destroying it.

Missouri shot 759 sixteen-inch projectiles during her Gulf War assignment, 611 of them during one sixty-hour period ending on 27 February. Her crew performed superbly in that period of about four days, spending most of it at general quarters and, for many of them, with little or no sleep.

Wisconsin became the Tomahawk missile Strike-warfare Centre during Operation Desert Storm and the last naval gunfire of that conflict came from her sixteen-inch main weapons. The Tomahawk and gunfire strikes, naval gunfire support in Kuwait, and the remotely piloted vehicle operations were all coordinated through *Wisconsin*. She acted as the Persian Gulf Force "over-the-horizon targetting coordinator", both at sea and in port. In February 1991 *Wisconsin* destroyed or inflicted severe damage on Iraqi communications facilities, special forces boats, artillery batteries, command posts, infantry bunkers, mechanized units, troop housing and surface-to-air missile sites. On 1 March, at Faylaka Island, the television camera of a *Wisconsin* RPV recorded the first instance of Iraqi troops waving white flags in an attempt to surrender to an unmanned aircraft. In her six months of service in the Gulf War, *Wisconsin* fired 324 sixteen-inch rounds, 881 five-inch rounds, 5,200 20mm rounds and launched twenty-four land-attack cruise missiles. She operated there without incurring a serious fire, flood or collision casualty or personnel injury.

right: Visitors to the USS *Arizona* memorial in Pearl Harbor as a flight of U.S. Navy F/A-18 Hornet fighters passes overhead. The battleship USS *Missouri* is in the background.

The nuclear suppercarrier USS *Carl Vinson* passing the battleship USS *Missouri* in Pearl Harbor.

The USS *Nevada* BB36 was one of the American battleships caught in Pearl Harbor by the Japanese aircraft of the 7 December 1941 attack. *Nevada* was the only battleship in the basin to get under way during the attack. She was hit by at least six bombs and one torpedo and had to be beached while trying to escape. She was later repaired and served as a convoy escort in the Atlantic and in a fire-support role in the invasion landings at Normandy, Southern France, Iwo Jima and Okinawa. She was later used in the atomic bomb tests at Bikini Atoll in 1946.

The German High Seas Fleet in the North Sea.

One of the Japanese vessels that fought in the Battle of Tsushima in May 1905.

Royal Navy battleship HMS *Dreadnought* in drydock; right: Admiral of the Fleet John Fisher, responsible for the construction of *Dreadnought*.

Left: Kapitän zur See Hans
Langsdorff of the German pocket
battleship *Graf Spee* (below).

The American "Great White Fleet."

HMS *Queen Mary*; right:
Admiral of the Fleet Sir
Henry Leach, RN Ret.

The superdreadnought HMS
Colossus.

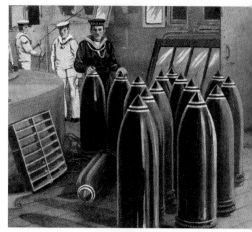

HMS *Revenge*; right: A happy homecoming in WW2.

left: The USS *Mississippi* BB23 in 1908; below: The USS *Louisiana* BB19 near Coronado, California.

Battleships in cinema:
below and right:
Tora,!Tora,!Tora!; bottom
left: *In Harm's Way*.

left: *Tora! Tora! Tora!*; bottom
right: *Under Siege*.

More cinema stills, these from *Sink The Bismarck* and, below: *Pursuit of the Graf Spee*; bottom right: *The Court Martial of Billy Mitchell*.

HMS *Hood* in 1932; right: A still from the film *Pearl Harbor*; centre right: The USS *California* burning in Pearl Harbor; far right: Impact point of a Kamikaze strike on the USS *Missouri*.

left: The *Arizona* Memorial in Pearl Harbor; below: The USS *Arizona* BB39, in Pearl Harbor drydock during 1939; above: The refloated hull of the USS *Oklahoma*.

left: A salvo from the *Missouri* in the Korean War; below: The USS *Texas* BB35; right: The *Iowa* BB61.

left: The USS *Alabama*;
below: The USS *Nevada*;
bottom: An American
reconnaissance floatplane;
bottom right: President
Harry S. Truman ran the
U.S. war effort in the last
months of WW2.

above: The USS *Wisconsin* berthed at the Naval Museum in Norfolk, Virginia; top centre: The *Bismarck* in a Norwegian fiord; top right: The USS *New Jersey*; below: The USS *Iowa*, July 1943; below right: HMS *Prince of Wales*.

PICTURE CREDITS: PHOTOS CREDITED TO THE AUTHOR'S COLLECTION ARE: AC; PHOTOS CREDITED TO THE U.S. NATIONAL ARCHIVES AND RECORDS ADMINISTRATION ARE: NARA; PHOTOS CREDITED TO THE U.S NAVY ARE: USN; PHOTOS CREDITED TO THE IMPERIAL WAR MUSEUM ARE: IWM; PHOTOS CREDITED TO THE ROYAL NAVY ARE: RN; PHOTOS CREDITED TO THE TAILHOOK ASSOCIATION ARE: TAILHOOK. P3-AC, P4 BOTH-AC, P5-AC, P6 BOTH-AC, P7-TAILHOOK, P8-AC, P10-USN, P11 BOTH-AC, P12-USN, P14-AC, P16-USN, P17-TONY IACONO, P20-AC, P21-AC, P23-AC, P24 BOTH-AC, P26-USN, P27-TAILHOOK, P29-AC, P30-AC, P31-AC, P32-USN, P35-P KAPLAN, P36-RN, P38-RN, P40 ALL-AC, P41 TOP-NARA, P41 BOTTOM-AC, P43 TOP-NARA, P43 BOTTOM BOTH-AC, P45 BOTH-AC, P46 TOP LEFT-E. WENDORF, P46 TOP RIGHT AND BOTTOM-AC, P47 TOP BOTH-AC, P47 BOTTOM-USN, P48-AC, P49-USN, P50-USN, P53 ALL-RN, P54-AC, P56 BOTH-AC, P57 TOP-AC, P57 BOTTOM-RN, P60-AC, P61-AC, P64-NARA, P66-TAILHOOK, P67-USN, P70-USN, P74 TOP AND BOTTOM RIGHT-NARA, P74 BOTTOM LEFT-P KAPLAN, P75 TOP-NARA, P75-P KAPLAN, P76-AC, P77-USN, P78-P KAPLAN, P80-AC, P82-AC, P86-AC, P90-AC, P94-AC, P97 BOTH-AC, P99-AC, P101-AC, P102-AC, P105-AC, P106-AC, P110-USN, P114-USN, P118-RN, P123-USN, P124-USN, P126-NARA, P128 TOP BOTH AND CENTRE-AC, P128 BOTTOM LEFT-IWM, P128 BOTTOM RIGHT-AC, P129 BOTH-AC, P130 TOP AND CENTRE-AC, P130 BOTTOM BOTH-P KAPLAN, P131 TOP AND BOTTOM LEFT-AC, P131 BOTTOM RIGHT-P KAPLAN, P132 ALL-AC, P133 ALL-AC, P134 TOP BOTH-20TH CENTURY FOX, P134 BOTTOM-PARAMOUNT, P135 TOP-20TH CENTURY FOX, P135 BOTTOM-WARNER BROS., P136 ALL-20TH CENTURY FOX, P137 TOP-THE RANK ORGANISATION, P137 BOTTOM LEFT-20TH CENTURY FOX, P137 BOTTOM RIGHT-WARNER BROS., P138 TOP LEFT-WRIGHT & LOGAN, P138 TOP RIGHT-TOUCHSTONE PICTURES/JERRY BRUCKHEIMER FILMS, P138 CENTRE AND BOTTOM-USN, P139 TOP LEFT AND CENTRE-AC, P139 TOP RIGHT-P KAPLAN, P139 BOTTOM-TAILHOOK, P140 ALL-AC, P141 TOP RIGHT AND CENTRE-AC, P141 BOTTOM LEFT-TAILHOOK, P141 BOTTOM RIGHT-NARA, P142 ALL-AC, P143 TOP-USN, P143 BOTTOM-IWM, P144 ALL-AC. GRATEFUL ACKNOWLEDGMENT IS MADE TO THE FOLLOWING FOR THE USE OF THEIR PREVIOUSLY PUBLISHED MATERIAL: GILBEY, JOSEPH, FOR EXTRACTS FROM HIS BOOK LANGSDORFF OF THE GRAF SPEE, PRINCE OF HONOUR, MASON, TED, FOR EXTRACTS FROM HIS BOOK BATTLESHIP SAILOR, NAVAL INSTITUTE PRESS, YOSHIDA, MITSURU, FOR EXTRACTS FROM HIS BOOK REQUIEM FOR BATTLESHIP YAMATO, UNIVERSITY OF WASHINGTON PRESS, WOUK, HERMAN, FOR AN EXTRACT FROM HIS BOOK THE CAINE MUTINY, JONATHAN CAPE LTD., THE ROYAL NAVY FOR EXTRACTS FROM THE BOOKLET YOUR SHIP, NOTES AND ADVICE TO AN OFFICER ON ASSUMING HIS FIRST COMMAND, HAINES, GREGORY, AND COWARD, B.R., FOR EXTRACTS FROM THEIR BOOK BATTLESHIP, CRUISER, DESTROYER.

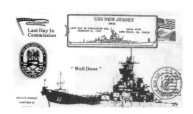